BE YOUR OWN BEST FRIEND

BE YOUR OWN BEST FRIEND

And other lessons from a life
in and out of the limelight

EKIN-SU CÜLCÜLOĞLU

PIATKUS

PIATKUS
First published in Great Britain in 2024 by Piatkus
1 3 5 7 9 10 8 6 4 2

Copyright © Ekin-Su Cülcüloğlu 2024

The moral right of the author has been asserted.

All rights reserved.
No part of this publication may be reproduced, stored in a retrieval system, or transmitted in any form or by any means, without the prior permission in writing of the publisher, nor be otherwise circulated in any form of binding or cover other than that in which it is published and without a similar condition including this condition being imposed on the subsequent purchaser.

A CIP catalogue record for this book
is available from the British Library.

ISBN 978-0-349-44007-1

All photographs from the author's collection.

Typeset in Palatino LT by Hewer Text UK Ltd, Edinburgh
Printed and bound in Great Britain by Clays Ltd, Elcograf S.p.A.

Papers used by Piatkus are from well-managed forests
and other responsible sources.

Piatkus
An imprint of
Little, Brown Book Group
Carmelite House
50 Victoria Embankment
London EC4Y 0DZ
An Hachette UK Company
www.hachette.co.uk

www.littlebrown.co.uk

To those who are feeling lost and learning how to be kind to themselves, this one is for you.

This book is a reminder of how wonderful you are. You deserve happiness and to see yourselves beyond the reflection in the mirror. You are worthy of feeling good enough, and I hope that you find love within.

This book is for you.

CONTENTS

Introduction: Ekin . . . who?   1

1 Don't let the bullies get you down   9
2 Inner beauty never goes out of style   29
3 You'll never be as young as you are right now   45
4 Keep hold of your dreams – and the rest will follow   65
5 Never let toxic relationships dim your glow   81
6 Always stay true to the real you   99
7 It's OK to struggle – even when you have 'everything'   121
8 Embrace the roller-coaster ride   147
9 Be your own best friend   171

Resources   182
Acknowledgements   183

Introduction

EKIN . . . WHO?

Have you ever felt like you're on top of the world one moment, only to come crashing down with a thump the next? I know I have.

In August 2022, I won a TV show called *Love Island*, alongside Davide, the boyfriend I had met (and was falling for) on the show. I have never experienced euphoria quite like the moment my name was called. The whole scene was like a dream. As I stood in the warm Mallorcan evening, the villa was lit up with twinkling fairy lights and neon hearts, and the lights from the cameras reflected off the sparkles on my dress. I was standing next to the man whom I genuinely believed I was going to marry; he held me close while we waited to find out if the public had voted for us to be their winners. My heart was beating so fast, and I had butterflies in my stomach. Whatever the outcome, I was going home with a new love – and I couldn't wait. When Laura Whitmore announced our names, I screamed and leapt into Davide's arms. I heard clapping from the crowd, and people shouting, 'We love you, Ekin-Su!' It was like I had entered a different universe. I hadn't just won this show – I had won my own life. Everything that had happened in my past no longer mattered. It felt like I had been reborn, and my life would only go up and up from here.

Fast-forward to March 2024, and I would be leaving yet another reality TV show – except this time, it wasn't such a euphoric experience. Fresh out of my break-up with Davide only a few weeks earlier, I sat on the big blue sofa in the *Celebrity Big Brother* house, listening to hosts AJ and Will read out the names of the housemates who had been nominated for eviction. When my name was called, I could hear booing from the crowds outside. I felt panic rising in my throat, and all I wanted to do was cry – but there was nowhere to hide, so I forced myself to smile.

Then I heard those infamous words: 'Ekin-Su, you have been evicted. Please leave the *Big Brother* house.' When I left the sliding doors of the house, I thought I might drown in the noise outside. I felt like I was desperately searching for a life raft. I had never felt so out of my depth, and so lost.

It's safe to say I have been through highs and lows since first stepping into the public eye. I experienced the most unbelievable love and support after leaving *Love Island*, and I was the subject of intense trolling and scrutiny after *Celebrity Big Brother* – and that's not even taking into account all the twists and turns with other TV shows and public dramas in between.

Living in the public eye is a bit like being on a roller coaster – you get the adrenaline rush of speeding down the track when everything is going well and people love you, but then there are moments when the ride feels broken or unstable, or like it's going off track, and you just want to get off because it's not fun any more. Experiencing both extremes has taught me some valuable lessons. It has reminded me that you can't be at the mercy of what other people think of you. You can't base your worth on whether other people love you or hate you, otherwise you'll lose yourself. You need to keep your feet firmly on the ground, and hold on tightly to your sense of self. In other words, you have to be your own best friend.

I know that my journey is a bit different, because these moments happened so publicly. But we've all had versions of this experience, haven't we? We've all felt loved and valued one minute, and down in the dumps the next. It's so easy to get swept up in the excitement of something – a new chapter, or a happily-ever-after – and then feel a lot of shame and self-blame when things get tough. But the thing is, every single person's life is a roller coaster. We all have incredible highs and terrible lows. The good news? It's *your* roller coaster. You can't always control how fast you go, or how many times you'll go upside down. But you *can* choose to look at your life with positivity and acceptance. You can hold your own hand, and learn to enjoy the ride. That's exactly what I am trying to do now – and it's why I'm writing this book.

You may have seen me on your TV screens over the past couple of years, and you might be wondering: who the hell is Ekin-Su? What do we actually know about her? Is she that confident bombshell who strutted into the *Love*

Island villa? A 'liar and actress'? Is she the one-dimensional girl we see on her social media channels, and on the cover of magazines? Or is she the cold, snappy girl from *Celebrity Big Brother*? The truth is, none of these versions of Ekin-Su tell the whole story. Opening up scares me – to be honest, I'm afraid of being misunderstood or hurt. But now feels like the right time to be vulnerable, and to show you the girl behind the newspaper stories, the reality TV shows and the filtered Instagram pictures. This book will be my safe space to open up, and I hope it encourages you to do the same.

Throughout my life, I have needed to rely on myself every step of the way. I was a lonely kid – bullied at school, and often alone at home – so I relied on my imagination and hopes for the future to comfort me. As a teenager, I fell victim to society's beauty standards, and changed myself as much as possible so that the world would think I was beautiful. I finally found validation for my looks through taking part in beauty pageants and having boyfriends, but I still felt ugly inside. Going to university and then moving to Turkey to chase my dreams of becoming an actress, I had to believe in myself and my goals despite setback after setback.

I haven't always got it right. Even though I have needed to be independent from a very young age, I have spent a lot of my life seeking approval and validation from other people. I have been in some unhealthy, toxic relationships that have worn me down and made me question my self-worth. I've looked for love and affection in all the wrong places, believing that everything would be fine if I could just get enough social media likes, bag the biggest work gig or fashion shoot, or find a man to love me like the ones I had watched in romcoms.

Of course, it's normal to want to be loved and accepted. I'm pretty sure *everyone* wants that. The problem comes when we are too reliant on other people and things to make ourselves happy. It's great to have supportive family, friends and romantic partners – but how can you expect other people to love and accept you when, deep down, you don't actually believe you're worthy of it?

In this book, I want to take you on the roller coaster of my life, through all the heartbreaks, loneliness and struggles, as well as the incredible moments that I have been lucky enough to experience. My life has been amazing in so many ways – I'm really grateful for everything I have. Still, I think it's important to be honest about the tough times, and to admit that life isn't perfect 100 per cent of the time. The pictures on Instagram doesn't always tell the whole story of what's going on behind the scenes. In the past, I haven't always been open, because there is so much pressure to be perfect. I have plastered a smile on my face and pretended everything was fine. I have called myself a strong, independent woman – when really, I was feeling vulnerable and scared. I have said 'yes' to opportunities because they sounded like a good idea, not because they were something I wanted. I have struggled with setting clear boundaries, and have allowed people to walk all over me.

Throughout all the highs and lows, I have learned a lot. And while I don't pretend to have all the answers, my hope is that these lessons might feel useful to you. Maybe you're in school right now, and my stories of not fitting in and how I found power in my authenticity will resonate with you. Maybe you've achieved a dream you've had since you were tiny, but you've realised it isn't everything you thought it would be. Or maybe you want to leave an unhappy relationship, but you're not sure whether it's the right decision. This book might be my story – but it's also *your* story. If you have ever felt like you're not good enough, then this is the book for you. If you've ever felt lost or misunderstood, then this is the book for you. If, despite your insecurities, you're still hopeful, open-hearted and have big goals and dreams, then this is the book for you. If you want to create a better relationship with yourself, then this is the book for you. Of course, I'm not a mental health expert or a scientist – I'm just an ordinary girl finding my way in the world, right alongside you. We're in it together.

As well as telling my story, I will offer some advice and share the lessons I've picked up along the way. Most importantly, I'll explain all the ways in which I have tried, and am still trying, to be the best friend that I've always longed for – to myself. The more you can learn about yourself, and the more you can find strength, acceptance and love from within, the happier you will be. I hope that this book will make you feel empowered to do just that – because the best friendship you'll ever have is the one you have with yourself.

Of course, I am not a perfect person, and my actions haven't always matched up with my words. It can be a lot easier to give advice, and much harder to put it into practice! I'm still learning as I go along, but that's OK. This is only the beginning . . .

Chapter 1

DON'T LET THE BULLIES GET YOU DOWN

For as long as I can remember, I've loved being the main character. When I was little, I would invite friends over to my house and insist we put on a play for my parents. We'd make up some kind of scenario – sometimes something as simple as two people meeting in a shop – and we'd put on an extravagant performance for my parents to film on their video camera.

I loved pretending to be different people. Whenever we went to Turkey to visit my grandparents and cousins, I'd dress up in my granddad's clothes (with a pillow stuffed inside my top to make it look like I had a big belly), draw on a moustache, and act like an old man. I was a real people-pleaser and loved making people laugh.

Looking back, I've always been quite dramatic too. I remember sometimes looking up at the stars in the sky, and feeling so inspired that I'd sing a song to myself. I viewed life as one big performance – the idea of singing, dancing and acting just put me in my element. I was a really confident child, and always believed I could make something of myself. 'When I grow up, I'm going to be famous,' I'd say to my family. They would laugh and roll their eyes, but my mum would always say, 'I'm sure you will be.'

My mum always remembers how confident I was when I was a little kid. She often tells a story about something that happened when I was five years old and we were on holiday in Ibiza. We were eating dinner and there was a flamenco dancer. Everyone was clapping for her, and I just thought, *I want people clapping for me*. So I ran off and got up on to one of the tables and started mimicking her dance moves. Everyone drifted away from the dancer towards me, clapping and giving me so much attention. I loved it.

On that same trip, my confidence even went so far as to cause a near-death experience. We were by the pool. My parents were sunbathing and I was watching all these older kids swimming, and I thought, *I want to do that*. I had this urge to do what they were doing, and I wasn't scared of the water, so I decided to jump in. The problem was, I couldn't actually swim, so I swallowed loads of water and sank to the bottom. It was terrifying, but thankfully a ten-year-old girl noticed my parents screaming, wondering where I was, and she swam down and rescued me. The next thing I knew, I was lying by the side of the pool, coughing and spluttering, while my mum was crying with relief that I was OK. It was obviously a very traumatic experience, but my mum always tells the story to remind me of how naturally brave I was. I always did what I wanted to do, without any fear.

* * *

I was lucky enough to have a lovely, supportive upbringing. My parents are both Turkish, and they met while studying for master's degrees at university. After they got married, they decided to pursue job opportunities in London – my mum as a teacher (and later a psychologist), and my dad as a graphic designer. Once they were settled in the UK, they had me, on 21 August 1994.

When I was little, it was just the three of us, and we lived in a small flat in Tottenham, north London. Both of my parents worked hard, so they couldn't always pick me up from school, and I'd often go to after-school clubs. I didn't mind, really; it was lonely sometimes, but it always instilled in me a desire to work hard and do what I love to the best of my ability. We lived in a multicultural area, so it was completely normal that I'd speak English at school and then go home and speak Turkish with my parents. I had friends from all over the world, from places like Albania and Jamaica. Everyone had their own cultures, and it was always interesting going round to my friends' houses and trying their foods and seeing their traditions. Everyone was different, but that was celebrated.

My parents knew how much I loved performing, so they signed me up for piano lessons (I got to Grade 5), and I'm incredibly grateful to my mum for sending me to ballet school from the age of five. There's something about dancing to classical music that I still adore now – it feels like flying. Performing shows like *Beauty and the Beast* and *Swan Lake* while wearing a sparkly tutu made me feel free. I felt like I could be myself. My teacher, Miss Pepper, always made me feel great about myself too.

She'd always say, 'You've got a stunning toe.' It sounds weird, but large big toes are actually useful for ballet, as they're good for pointing your feet. I looked at her like a second mother figure, because she made me believe I was good at something. Even at such a young age, I recognised how nice it felt to be acknowledged.

When Everything Changed

When I got to year five, my parents had two very big pieces of news for me. The first bit of news was that my mum was pregnant – I was going to have a baby brother! This part wasn't so bad. I had always wanted a sibling, as I felt lonely quite a lot. Still, I was worried about what it might mean for me. I loved being the centre of attention – would a new baby change that? Would I get left behind?

But the other piece of news was much worse: we were moving away from everything I had known in Tottenham. My parents had bought a bigger house in Essex, they said, with a lovely garden and lots of room to play. They tried to make it sound appealing, but all I could think about was how I'd have to leave my school, and all my friends, who felt like my family since we spent so much time together. I'd also have to stop my piano lessons, and move away from my lovely ballet teacher. When you're eight years old, news like that can feel like the end of the world. My life in Tottenham was all I knew. On my last day at school, I remember crying buckets. I cried to my teachers and my friends. It felt like my life was over! But then I went home to my parents, including my now heavily pregnant mum, and made out like nothing was wrong. I wanted them to feel like I was good at handling things.

When moving day arrived, I had managed to convince myself that maybe moving to Essex wouldn't be so bad after all. And I was really excited when I saw the house – it was much bigger than our old flat. I couldn't wait to design my room. I loved the Groovy Chick brand, and wanted it to be all pink and fluffy. Some of our neighbours came to introduce themselves and say hello, and everyone seemed really friendly. I was so taken aback by the Essex accents – it was the first time I'd heard them. They had all kinds of slang words that I'd never heard before, like saying someone was being 'salty' if they were acting weird. I knew it was something I'd have to get used to, but I believed that I would find my feet.

When the first day at my new primary school arrived, I was all ready to go, dressed in my long skirt, with a Nike backpack (the most popular bag back in Tottenham) and my Bratz dolls lunchbox. When my dad dropped me off at school, I was absolutely terrified. *What if nobody likes me?* I thought. *What if I don't fit in?*

'Come on, Ekin. You can do this,' I told myself, and went into my class.

Sadly, my worst fears came true – and quickly. I looked around the classroom and got a very distinct feeling that I didn't belong there. For starters, almost everyone was white and blond. It was very different from my previous school, where everyone looked so different, and most people had parents from different countries. Here, I stood out like a sore thumb. Then I noticed how mature the girls looked. We were only in year six, but some of them were already wearing full faces of make-up. Their school skirts were all much shorter than mine, and the bags they were carrying were from Chanel, D&G and other designer brands. I didn't know at the time just how expensive these bags were, but I could tell this was a new kind of 'cool' – a far cry from the sports bags and fashion that I was used to in Tottenham – and I definitely wasn't part of it.

Then came time for the teacher to go through the register. I knew the name Ekin-Su was different, but it had never mattered at my old school, where lots of people's names were interesting. Here, everyone had very British names: Hannah, Sarah, Tom, Dan. Then, the teacher reached my name: 'Ekin-Su'. Everyone started laughing. My cheeks went bright red.

'Oh my god, are you Chinese?' one person said, and I struggled to understand why that would even be an insult.

'Ekin-*Poo*,' said someone else.

I had never felt so embarrassed, and I vowed that I would change my name to Sue. I wanted to use a British name, as I hoped it would make me feel more accepted.

But the damage was done: I was well and truly an outsider here. One day, I was wandering around the school on my own and I overheard some of the girls talking about a party they were going to on the weekend. I thought to myself: *This is how I make friends. I need to throw a party!* So my mum allowed me to throw a Halloween party, and I invited all the kids from school. Back in London, when we were planning Halloween costumes, the rule was always: the scarier, the better. So I decided to go as a creepy devil, wearing a long red dress, horns and face-paint. When the girls started arriving, it was honestly like that famous scene in *Mean Girls*. They were all dressed as cats and bunny rabbits, looking more pretty than scary. I remember thinking: *They're all so beautiful, and I'm just a monster*. But the party wasn't so bad; everyone seemed to enjoy it, and people actually talked to me for once. I thought I had finally done it. I had made friends, and now I would fit in.

The Monday after, I couldn't wait to sit with my friends at lunchtime – but they all acted like they didn't know me again. I'd go up to people in the playground and say, 'Hey,' and they'd act like they didn't know who I was. They'd all eat their lunch together, but I knew I wasn't welcome, so I would go and eat my lunch on my own in a toilet cubicle. It was so depressing, biting into my sandwich while reading all the graffiti on the back of the door, hearing the sounds of giggling girls outside. It makes me choke up thinking about it, to be honest with you. But I also felt a weird sense of safety inside that cubicle too, like I knew I wouldn't be judged in there.

Occasionally, I would summon up the courage to try and get involved, but it would usually backfire. One lunchtime, I went up to one of the prettiest, most popular girls, and offered her my sandwich. *Maybe if I share something, they'll invite me into the group*, I thought.

But she picked up my sandwich, opened it up and threw it at me.

I was stunned. 'Why did you do that?' I asked.

'You're a Turk – go back to your own country,' she said. Then she pushed me on to the concrete and said, 'You belong on the floor.'

Everyone else stood by and laughed. I could feel the tears welling but I didn't want to give them the satisfaction of knowing they had hurt me, so I ran away and cried quietly in the loos.

I don't think I recognised that it was bullying at the time – I just thought there must be something wrong with me. I also didn't tell my parents what I was going through. My mum had complications with her pregnancy, so she had to stay in hospital for twenty days before my baby brother was born. My dad was doing all the drop-offs and pick-ups, and we'd go and visit my mum in the hospital after school. I didn't want to give them anything else to worry about. Even at that young age, I felt a lot of shame and embarrassment about what was happening. I didn't want them to think that their daughter – who was usually so confident and loved being the centre of attention – wasn't liked by anyone. My parents would ask me how school was going, and I'd smile brightly and tell them I was enjoying it. I didn't want them to think I was a loser. I just wanted them to be proud of me.

Instead, I tried to distract myself as best I could when I was at home – it was my safe haven. I would spend my £3 weekly pocket money on chocolate and sweets, and I'd go home and sit in front of the TV watching Nickelodeon. It's so sad to say it, but snacks were my friends during that time. It's no wonder that I ended up putting on weight; I became the 'chubby' kid, and got bullied even more relentlessly. It was a vicious cycle: the unhappier I was, the more I ate – but more on that later.

Things started looking up when my brother, Arda, was born. I was completely obsessed with him. I remember visiting him for the first time at the hospital – he had to stay in an incubator for three days. He was so small and skinny, and he had a full head of hair that looked like a hairball. I thought, *Wow, this is my brother. Finally, I will have a friend!* When he came home, I would spend all my time pinching and squeezing his face. I felt like I had a bond with him. Even though he was a tiny baby, I felt like I could tell him things that I couldn't tell my parents. I'd tell him about what I was doing in school, and about the mean kids in class. He was almost like a soft toy – he obviously couldn't say anything back, but I felt comforted by his presence.

It also helped that I finally made a friend in school. A few weeks after I arrived, we found out that another new person would be arriving. I thought, *I won't be the weird new one any more!*

When Lucy walked into the classroom, I knew immediately that we would be friends (I've changed her name for her privacy). For starters, she looked like a normal nine-year-old – no perfect make-up or designer handbags – which meant she'd stick out at our school, just like me. The teacher sat her next to me, and I introduced myself as Sue. Straight away, I noticed her dorky laugh (which was just like mine), and she confessed how much she loved chocolate and sweets – just like me. She told me about her complicated family life, and I realised straight away that she needed a friend. Instinctively, I decided I would be a good friend to her – because I knew what it felt like to be on your own.

From that point onwards, we were inseparable. I would invite her round to my house and we'd watch *Zoey 101* (my favourite show) and eat loads of snacks. I would go round to her house, too, which wasn't too far away. They'd always eat really English meals, like pie, and sausages and mash, and I loved feeling like part of English culture. Clearly, Lucy had her own traumas, and people at school didn't seem to 'get' her either, so we found comfort in our own little bubble.

The Dreaded Teenage Years

When it came time to apply for secondary school, Lucy and I were looking forward to starting our new lives in year seven. We were both going to Roding Valley High School in Loughton, Essex. Although it's a state school, the catchment area is full of big houses with huge driveways and automatic gates, so lots of the kids who go there are extremely wealthy. I knew that a lot of the kids from our primary school would be going there, but I also knew that it was a much bigger school, and there would be more opportunities to make new friends. I was really excited to start.

Lucy and I went to get our school uniforms together. Unlike the other girls, who would have their skirts tailored to be shorter, we both had strict parents, so we had long skirts, and blazers were bought a few sizes bigger so that we could grow into them. The first day of high school, I found out I was in the same form as Lucy.

It felt so good to have an ally this time. But as soon as the names on the register were called, all the trauma came flooding back. I hadn't told my parents I was going by Sue, so my real name ended up in the register, and once again there was laughter.

'Who the fuck calls their child Ekin-Su?' I heard someone ask.

The feeling of not being accepted smacked me in the face – all the bullying and name-calling came flooding back, and I knew I wasn't going to escape it in this school either. If anything, I knew it was probably going to get worse. In that moment, I wished I was someone else. I wanted to have blond hair, and a normal name. I looked at the other girls in the class and wished we could trade places.

This time, though, I decided there was no point in wasting time trying to get people to like me. I had Lucy, so I just wanted to focus on other things that made me happy. Mostly, that was performing. I was always the most excited for my Drama lessons. In every single lesson, the teacher would say, 'Who's up first?' and I'd run to the centre of the room. For some reason, I didn't really care what people thought of me in those classes. Even when people laughed at me, I still felt so confident acting, and enjoyed every minute of it. People would say, 'You look ridiculous, you're so ugly, you're so fat,' but I just ignored them. When I was acting, their words would wash over me – because in those moments, I wasn't me. I was someone much more confident and self-assured. Sometimes, it can be easier to pretend you're someone else.

I wasn't the most academic of teenagers, but my lessons were another welcome distraction from my severe lack of a social life. I loved my History classes. Learning about the past fascinated me.

I also loved English. I guess it was similar to Drama in the way that it offered that element of escapism – you could get lost in stories, and dive deeply into understanding why people felt the way they did. My favourite book we studied was *Holes* by Louis Sachar – to this day, I still think it's such a clever story, and the movie is so good too. Even though I wasn't the best at English, my teacher, Miss Flynn, noticed how interested I was in her classes, and she took me under her wing. I loved how she spoke with such passion – it inspired me to be passionate about things too. She wanted to help me improve my grammar, so I would go and see her after school, and she'd encourage me to read different books and look at interesting quotes. I really felt like I had a friend in her.

Chatting to teachers was enjoyable for me. I must've been the only kid in the school who would say hello to them, or bring them an apple and ask how they were. But it's because the teachers were always nicer to me than other kids were. I also found that I felt more comfortable around older people – I think it was because I had been an only child for the first eight years of my life. It never really bothered me hanging out with people's parents or spending lunchtimes with the teachers. I've always believed that older people are wiser, and there's so much you can learn from them. This definitely made me seem even weirder to the other kids, who would taunt me for being a teacher's pet.

It took me many years to unpack why I was picked on so much. Getting on with teachers was just one reason why I was different from other kids, but there were lots of other reasons too. There was the fact I was Turkish. There was the fact my strict parents wouldn't let me have a mobile phone as early as everyone else, and the fact I always had to wear the longer skirts and baggier school blazers. As I got older, my personal style became more 'emo' – I had my fringe cut to the side and would apply dark eyeliner and black nail polish. I was into eighties music, like ABBA and Freddie Mercury. My style was different to the other kids in my school, who preferred fake tan and white stilettos. Of course, there's nothing wrong with that look if that's what you're into. But I think people had such a big problem with me because, even in the face of the relentless bullying, I refused to back down and become something I wasn't. I was always going to like the things I liked, and do the things I enjoyed, and if that meant everyone hated me – so be it. And I think, in a way, that confidence in itself is a reason for kids to take issue with you.

On one occasion, the headteacher asked me if I'd like to perform in an assembly as all the kids were entering the hall. I decided to sing and play piano to 'Hello' by Lionel Richie. With every line I sang, I felt like I was really expressing my emotions, telling people subliminally to stop being cruel to me, and that I just wanted to be happy. When I sat down, everyone laughed at me and mocked me. Someone said: 'You're so embarrassing for doing that.'

But I knew that, just because I would never be acknowledged and appreciated by the kids at my school, it didn't mean I would never be acknowledged and appreciated ever. My time would come.

Fighting Loneliness

With the absence of party invitations and a big friendship group, I found comfort and community on the internet. When I was in high school, it was all about MSN Messenger. You could add the people in your class, but you could also add random people, so I would speak to all sorts of people on there. I remember putting the lyrics to sad songs in my 'MSN status' when I was feeling sad, as a way to send subtle messages to my contacts list about how I was feeling (a bit like posting an 'indirect' Instagram story nowadays). I also used Myspace (which was perfect for emo kids like me), but my favourite was Habbo Hotel. It was basically a virtual cartoon hotel, where you could make a character, then explore the different rooms of the hotel and meet people. Lucy and I would sit on my family computer by the front door (computers were always in communal areas back then), and chat to random people on Habbo Hotel. It was fun, because they didn't know who we were, and they didn't judge us based on who we were at school. We could be anything we wanted to be.

Looking back now, it was pretty bad that we had access to these sites. I remember once speaking to a man who initially lied about his age. He asked us where we lived, and we naively told him. He asked us to go on MSN and put the webcam on. We did, but then it immediately felt wrong, so we stopped and deleted him from everything. After that, we realised we needed to be careful. Just because the internet seemed like a safer place than the school playground, it didn't mean it actually was. But still, we liked to talk to people online – that was our social life. My parents hated me being on the internet, though, so I'd log on while they were at work, keeping my eye on the window to spot their cars pulling into the driveway.

To be honest, I was lonely a lot of the time. Even though I had Lucy and Arda and my parents, I spent a lot of time on my own, making up performances and dreaming about the future, when people would give me the positive attention and respect I knew I deserved. But, in a weird way, I actually think loneliness served me well. I learned a lot by being on my own. When you're around people all the time, you can become easily influenced. In school, the popular groups all did the same things – they all wore the same clothes and listened to the same music. Because I wasn't really included in that anyway, I thought, *What's the point?* I might as well follow my own path.

Of course, I would never diminish the importance of having supportive people around you. But I do think there's something to be said for being on your own every once in a while. It builds independence. It makes you less reliant on other people. All those years I spent feeling lonely have made me stronger.

Bullying is Never About You

If you were bullied or felt like an outsider in school, you'll probably know that the trauma can stay with you for years afterwards. It can make you untrusting and fearful around other people. This happened to me when I first moved to Turkey in my twenties – even though I was going 'home', I felt like an outsider again because I was British. It was like being that weird teenager again.

And I was transported back to that feeling on *Love Island*. There was a moment where I felt surrounded by the girls in the group. One of them seemed to have a problem with me – she was suggesting that I'm fake. It took me by surprise how quickly it sent me back to feeling like that sad, scared girl who no one liked in school. I had come on to *Love Island* as a bombshell, more confident than ever; I'd never have thought in a million years that I'd be back in that frame of mind. The younger me would have run away and not said anything. But I thought to myself: *No. I am older now. I am wiser. I have been through enough to know my self-worth and to never allow people to walk all over me again.* Although I felt like I was a child again, I wanted to win this situation on behalf of the younger Ekin. So I asked this woman what exactly her problem was, and watched her come up with answers that didn't seem to make sense.

And that's when I realised. When someone picks on you, it's never actually about you – not really. It has everything to do with their own insecurities, their own anxieties, their own traumas. Sometimes, they pick at a flaw in you because it's something that feels threatening to their own sense of self. I think I had always known this, deep down, and that's why I always carried on being myself in school despite all the shit that was thrown my way. But now it felt even more obvious. I was never going to let another person make me feel worthless again. So I stayed calm and I didn't let them bring me down. And clearly, so many of you supported me and backed me 100 per cent. I'm so grateful for that.

Bullying can happen at any point in life. Some people think it only happens in school – and, of course, kids can be incredibly mean – but really, bullying can happen at any time. Maybe you have a colleague who is constantly putting you down, or a relative who goes out of their way to make you feel terrible. The first step towards feeling better is just remembering that the problem is with them, not with you. When you feel that anger or sadness rising in your body, transform it into pity. They must be extremely unhappy to want to make *you* unhappy. It's true what they say that 'hurt people hurt people'. Now, when someone is being mean to me, I just think, *They're not OK, and I feel sorry for them*. Instead of screaming at them, I think about how much they need a hug. It's amazing how this simple mindset shift can stop the bullying from having such a hold on you.

The next step is to tell someone what you're experiencing. It's normal to feel shame when you're being bullied, and to want to deny that it's a problem. I know, because this is exactly what I did when I was in school. Looking back, I wish I had told my mum and dad about what I was going through. It would have really helped to get it out in the open, and I'm sure they would've had some great advice. When I told them everything many years later, they were so sad that I hadn't confided in them. They loved me so much, and never would've thought I was a loser, or felt ashamed of me. I understand that now. You shouldn't have to deal with something alone. Speak to someone you trust. You're not weak for admitting you need help. I wish I could go back and tell that to my younger self.

I also wish I had stood up to my bullies more. I know it's easier said than done to speak up, especially when the person bullying you is more powerful, or bigger in some way. So I think the first step is to build your own self-confidence – to remind yourself that your voice is worth just as much as theirs. To remember that you believe in yourself, even if they don't. That you have enough inner strength to not care what they think.

In the next chapters, I'll go into more detail about the different ways in which you can build your self-worth, but one thing that I find helpful is to stand in front of the mirror every morning when I wake up and say to my reflection: 'I am enough.'

Ultimately, bullying is designed to take away your self-worth and make you feel insecure. If you're already insecure, this will make you feel even worse. But if you work on growing a strong sense of self, then you'll be much more resilient to any insults they hurl at you. Remember that you are unique; there is no one else quite like you in the world. The things some people hate you for will ultimately become the things other people will love you for. I am living proof of that.

Experiencing bullying is horrible. It leaves you with anxiety, paranoia and panic. It can make you feel like you're broken inside. But I also think anyone who goes through these hard times knows that you do come out the other side – and you become a better person for it. Being bullied has made me more empathetic. I think it's made me so much better at understanding what other people are going through, and I know that there's always more going on than meets the eye. I think I have become very good at reading people. And I have also learned that I can get through hard times. I know that I will always have myself to rely on.

The fact is, you're born alone and you die alone. That sounds morbid, but the more you can embrace that, the better. You learn to care less about what other people think of you. You learn to let their words and criticisms completely wash over you. You learn to find your true people: the people who get you, and make you feel good about yourself. You learn that your own aspirations, dreams, hobbies and morals are more important than what other people think of you. The bullies are always gonna bully – but you can just keep on being you.

Chapter 2

INNER BEAUTY NEVER GOES OUT OF STYLE

I think every girl has a moment in their teens when they suddenly transform the way they look. Mine was triggered by having a crush. I'm not even sure I can remember his name, but I do know I was obsessed with him. I was about fourteen years old, and he was in the year above me. He was tall and played basketball in the playground, and he had spiky mousy-brown hair. Whenever I saw him, I felt adrenaline from my feet to my head. It felt like I couldn't breathe.

We had never actually spoken – in fact, he had never even acknowledged my existence. I knew I needed to get him to look at me. I observed the kinds of girls he would talk to, and I thought: *I need to make myself look like them.* Of course, there were some things that I couldn't change (especially at that age), like my skin tone and my hair colour. What I could change was a part of me that had been a source of my bullying for years: my weight.

At that time, I felt a lot of pressure to be slim. All the images I saw in the magazines and on my favourite TV shows showed women who were very small. I desperately wanted to look like Zoey from *Zoey 101* – I wanted her hair, and all her clothes, which seemed to fit perfectly on her smaller frame. The ultimate idea of beauty seemed to be being as slim as possible. I wasn't huge, but, thanks to all the snacks I ate to make myself feel happier, I was slightly overweight. And I knew that, in order to get the attention of the boy I liked (and also feel more accepted at school), I would need to stop being 'fat'.

So I came home from school one day and googled 'how to lose weight in two weeks'. I'm not going to tell you the specific crash diet I tried, because I don't want to encourage anyone else to do what I did. It was extremely unhealthy, and I would never recommend that kind of diet to anyone. But I also think it's important to be honest. I was young, and really didn't know any better at the time. I saw someone talking about an incredibly restrictive diet in an online forum, and I decided to give it a go. It was extremely minimal – it centred around mostly eating fruit and drinking water. I somehow managed to avoid mealtimes, and my parents, who were constantly busy, didn't seem to notice that I was eating differently. It didn't make me feel good. I noticed I was angry all the time, and I was constantly picking fights with my family. After about a month, I knew I had to stop – but by that point, the weight had already fallen off. Looking in the mirror, I really liked what I saw. I had more definition in my cheekbones, and I felt confident enough to start wearing short skirts. Eating that way was horrible, but I'll be honest with you – liking my appearance felt addictive.

This happened at about the same time that school was breaking up for summer. My family travelled over to

Turkey to spend time with my grandparents and cousins like we always did. My trips to Turkey were always pretty healthy in terms of eating – lots of good food, olive oil and tomatoes. I felt much better eating that way than I had on the crash diet. Plus, one of my cousins was part of a marathon running club, and she invited me along. I had never even run a kilometre before, but I thought running could make me look even more trim, so I decided to give it a try. I remember the first day we went. The sun was beating down, and I felt so out of breath after one lap. But then I thought, *I'll just do another one.* Before I knew it, I was getting such a thrill from the running. I couldn't stop! I know so many people run to help themselves lose weight, and that was definitely my initial reason for doing it, but I didn't realise how euphoric it can make you feel. I loved it.

On that same trip, my auntie suggested I go for a haircut. I asked for caramel highlights (just like Zoey from *Zoey 101*) and when it was done, I looked in the mirror and couldn't recognise myself. I was tanned, with great hair, and I felt slim – it was such an amazing feeling. It was interesting to notice how quickly the attention I received shifted. Leaving the salon, I noticed people looking at me as I walked past. It gave me that feeling of validation and acknowledgement I had always chased. Looking back, I realise I was focused so much on my external self that I started to pay less attention to who I was inside. I had begun to believe that self-worth was measured by how I looked, and how skinny I could be. I was beginning to lose my true self – who I really was, beyond my appearance.

Preparing to go back to school, I bought some make-up and started straightening my hair (which was all the rage at the time). When I arrived at school for my first day of year ten, I strutted in like someone out of one of my favourite romcoms. Suddenly, the bullies who had always insulted me started whistling at me. I had never had that kind of attention from the opposite sex before, and it felt good. And then, that first week, I went up to the boy I had that overwhelming crush on.

'Hi,' he said. 'Are you new here? I haven't seen you before.'

I thought, *Oh my god, this is a joke.* I couldn't believe it. As much as I was happy about my new-found attention, I couldn't help feeling bad for my past self. Why hadn't I deserved respect and validation just as I was? I hadn't really changed inside.

As it happened, I had already gone off him by this point. As is the way with teenage crushes, it went just as quickly as it arrived. It wasn't really him that mattered, anyway. It was the idea that he would see me, and want me. Mission accomplished.

Of course, I enjoyed this new feeling. It was nice to finally feel valued for my appearance. The problem was, the insecurity was always there, just below the surface. Even when people told me I was pretty, there was still a little voice telling me that I was fat and that I wasn't good enough. I would only realise later on that happiness has to come from the inside. You can't just change your appearance and then expect it to solve all your problems. You don't need to change the way you look to be accepted you deserve to feel accepted regardless.

That said, once I had passed the very unhealthy phase of the crash diet, my new habits that were focused around my appearance did serve me well. I carried on running when I got back from Turkey, and I tried to keep my diet as fresh and healthy as possible. I still enjoyed my snacks, but I started finding more value in healthy salads and vegetables. To be honest, I think that's a normal part of growing up. You start to realise which habits are working for you, and which aren't. Making these changes meant I had so much more energy. I wasn't just sitting on the sofa all day any more – I wanted to get outside. It made me a lot more active, and the mental health benefits were even better than the physical benefits. I still didn't know the ins and outs of nutrition and fitness – all of that came later. But I did know that I felt better when I ate more fruit and veg and moved more. It just shows that moving your body and eating well has much more value when you're doing it to feel good, rather than to look good (but we'll go into that in more detail later).

Becoming a Beauty Queen

When I was fifteen years old, I was out shopping when a woman stopped me in the street. 'You're beautiful,' she said. 'Have you ever thought about doing beauty pageants?'

My knowledge of pageants came from one of my favourite romcoms (*Miss Congeniality*) and the TV show *Toddlers & Tiaras*, where little kids in the USA wore frilly dresses and tons of make-up to win cash prizes. I didn't even know that pageants were a thing in the UK, but I was flattered and it sounded fun, so I asked her what it would entail.

Now, I know what you're thinking: it's a scam! But, actually, it wasn't. The woman was a talent scout. She gave me her card and told me to get back to her, so I did some research with my parents later that evening. It was all legitimate, and the woman said she could get me sponsorship from a jewellery company to compete in a small local pageant that was held in a London club. If I won this one, she said, I could compete in a global pageant called the Miss Asia Pacific, representing one of the countries in the UK. It sounded like an adventure, and my parents said they'd support me if I wanted to do it.

A few months later, I was gearing up for my first pageant. I was told about all the different rounds I'd need to prepare for: there was a bikini round, and another round where we had to wear a long black dress. I was sponsored, so thankfully I didn't have to pay for anything myself, and it was so much fun picking out my outfits and trying them on. There was also an interview round, where I had to think about what makes a good beauty queen, a talent round (I chose to sing), and there was also a requirement to do some charity work in local organisations. But despite these extra elements, the pageant was still very much focused on how you looked. Image was everything. You were expected to be perfect in every way, but you especially had to *look* perfect. For me, there was something very validating about walking down that runway and having people who were judging me for how I looked mark me positively. Because even though I enjoyed my new-found beauty, I still felt like that insecure girl inside. I couldn't believe it when they called my name (I was going by Susie Hayzel) as second runner-up. I won a crown. Technically, it wasn't much but, for me, it represented approval.

That first pageant was such a fun experience. I loved having my hair and make-up done – it made me feel like a celebrity. And I loved the feeling of being on stage – it was like acting, in a way. You had to give the judges what they wanted, walking gracefully and smiling on cue. It felt like a real turning point for me. I had gone from being bullied for my looks, to being celebrated for them. It was addictive, and I was so excited to go and compete in the next stage of the competition: the Miss Asia Pacific, which was being held in Seoul in South Korea.

I was only seventeen years old when I travelled to Seoul, without either of my parents. Instead, I was chaperoned by a woman manager. Technically, they weren't supposed to allow anyone under eighteen to take part in the pageant, but no one checked my date of birth. We flew out there for two weeks, and it was such an exciting adventure. I hadn't travelled anywhere further than Turkey before, and Seoul was like a whole different world. It felt like I was in a movie. I remember walking into a Starbucks and it having a completely different menu – I bought a matcha tea and thought I was so cool. I was fascinated by the heated toilet seats, and robots that would offer toilet tissue in the loos. The culture was so different too. I remember at the hotel, all the other girls were kicking off because only men were allowed in the hotel gym. 'Where's our gym?!' I remember them saying. Women didn't seem to have the same freedoms at that time. But I found it so exciting being in such a different environment.

Thanks to winning my pageant, I was assigned to be Miss Ireland – even though I had never been there in my life! It was a bit strange, but it was fascinating meeting all the other girls from around the world. They were all so beautiful. I remember meeting Miss Russia and Miss Venezuela, and being wowed by how stunning they were. But there was also a darker side to the pageants if you looked beneath the surface. They were extremely competitive. Now, I'm not saying there's anything wrong with that, but sometimes it was taken too far. I heard stories about a jealous girl sneaking into another girl's room to spray-paint her heels a different colour just before the pageant, to sabotage her.

Most of all, though, I noticed how unhappy so many of these girls were. All many of them cared about was appearance, and whether their dresses would fit right on the night. This meant that many of them had unhealthy eating habits – and quite a few had eating disorders. The problem was, this was encouraged in the pageant world. I would load up my bowl with ice cream at the hotel buffet, and my manager at the time would tell me to eat an apple or a carrot instead. I noticed that all the girls skipped carbs, eating only meat and salads and ignoring the chips and pastas I was drawn to. I went along with it because I wanted to do the pageant 'right'. I thought: *Is this OK?* Eating less food made me feel depressed, and reminded me of that crash diet I'd done a few years before. I felt restricted, and it took some of the shine away from staying in this new city and this swanky hotel, getting up on stage each night for the different rounds and being the centre of attention, which I loved. But I wanted to do a good job, and if that meant eating less, so be it. I saw the lengths some of the girls would go to in order to look smaller. One night, before one of the rounds, I noticed another competitor making herself sick. I knew I didn't want to go down that path, but I was still so unkind to my body.

In the end, I came fifteenth out of seventy-five countries. I was pretty proud of myself, and when I got home, I competed in a few more pageants. But eventually, I knew I needed to focus more on college and invest my time in what I really wanted to pursue: acting. Looking back, I did really enjoy my pageant experience. It really brought me out of my shell, and allowed me to travel to exciting parts of the world and meet new people. But I think that, even though a competition can validate you and make you feel pretty, it can also do the opposite. You end up looking around and comparing yourself to other beautiful people, and suddenly the pressure to look a certain way (which only fits a very narrow ideal of beauty) becomes all-consuming.

Although I didn't stay in pageants for that long, this feeling would end up becoming a recurring theme later in my life – first as a singer and actor, then appearing on some of Britain's biggest reality TV shows. In all the work I have done, image plays a huge role, and it's easy to be convinced that how you look is absolutely the most important thing. You can get sucked into being completely obsessed by your appearance. But I have seen first-hand that the most beautiful person in a room is rarely the happiest or most confident.

Chasing Perfection is a Losing Game

Look, I'm not going to pretend that my appearance isn't important to me at all. I really enjoy the process of making myself look nice. I take the time with my skincare routine, morning and night, partly because I want my skin to glow, but partly because it feels good to make that time for myself. I also find doing my make-up so therapeutic. Blending eyeshadow and choosing the nicest lipstick colour is fun for me. In fact, I'd even go so far as to say that the best part of going to an event is getting dolled up. I know some people can't be arsed getting ready – and yes, it's a lot of effort, especially when you're fake-tanning and curling your hair or whatever. But I'm not doing it for the paparazzi guy. I do it because I genuinely really enjoy it.

I know it's hard to draw the line between what you actually like, and what you do because you think you are supposed to. Sometimes putting on make-up can be a bit like putting on a mask. I don't think anyone should ever feel like they need to wear make-up or dress a certain way. It felt so restrictive when I was at school that all the girls wore the same things and had their hair the same way – and to be honest, that continues into adult life too. In my industry, there's a certain pressure to look the same as everyone else. I'm not saying I don't give in to that pressure sometimes. It's no secret that I've had Botox and lip fillers in the past, and I'm not ashamed to say that. I have also had a boob job, which has left me with physical scars. I do think you should have the freedom to do what you want with your appearance and not be shamed for it.

But it's important to do it for the right reasons. Is it because seeing other people's wrinkle-free foreheads and plump lips makes you feel bad about yourself? Because if so, you should question that. You should only make changes to the way you look because you want to, not because other people make you feel like you should.

I've realised that chasing a specific idea of beauty is pointless. It's funny: when I was younger, I was desperate to look older. Now that I'm older, I want to look younger. The grass is always greener on the other side, and you'll always want what you can't have. For example, people with curly hair want straight hair, and people with straight hair want curly hair. The problem is, we look around at other people too much, rather than looking at ourselves and who we are inside.

Also, 'beautiful' is an ever-changing idea, and it's a lot to do with what's going on in society and culture in a given moment. When I was younger, there was a very skinny supermodel ideal, but then it changed to the Kardashian look of the noughties: a curvier figure and fuller lips. Ideas of what looks most attractive are constantly changing – everything goes out of style, then comes back in again. It can be fun changing your make-up according to the latest trends, but making huge changes to what you actually look like is a losing battle. To be completely honest, I regret some of the work I have had done. Now, I'm trying to embrace my natural beauty a lot more. Do I wish I had loved my appearance without the tweaks? Yes, I do. I can't go backwards, though. All I can do is think carefully about these kinds of decisions moving forward. Instead of changing myself to fit the trends, I want to stay true to who I am. Being authentic never goes out of style.

But I get it; everywhere we turn, we feel the pressure to look a certain way. Social media – especially Instagram and TikTok – is a big part of this. If you scroll on your favourite influencer's page, you'll see pictures of them looking absolutely flawless – and it can make you feel bad about yourself. I feel it too. And I think that it's OK to want to look nice on social media, and it's OK to have fun with filters. But it's important to remember that this isn't real life. Just because that influencer is posting pictures of herself looking airbrushed and glamorous, doesn't mean she's not also spending her evening in bed with her hair all over the place, wearing mis-matching pyjamas, with her face covered in pimple patches. You should also remember that if she's a full-time influencer, she might have access to expensive gyms and trainers, facials and skincare – so it's not a realistic standard everyone can live up to. And despite all that, she's probably just as insecure as you. It's so easy to see other people's pictures and think we're not good enough, but ultimately, we're all dealing with different versions of the same stuff.

You Are Beautiful! Yes, You!

You know how great it is when someone pays you a compliment? Whether it's a friend or a stranger in a nightclub bathroom, being told that you look nice can give you such a boost. But you don't need to wait for someone else to validate you – you can actually do that for yourself. 'Affirmations' – saying something nice about yourself, to yourself – can genuinely shift your mindset. I remember one day, I was feeling really down on myself. I'd been on a date that didn't go so well, and it really rocked my confidence. So, I looked in the mirror and said: 'I am beautiful. I'm great. I love myself.' It felt weirdly good, so I repeated it five times over. At first, this felt strange and maybe a little self-indulgent. But I'm learning that I will always be my biggest cheerleader – nobody else.

So many of us associate physical attractiveness with confidence, but I have learned that we get confidence from so many different places. Maybe you are absolutely hilarious, and you light up every room with your humour. Perhaps you are a boss at your job, and everyone in your office looks up to you. Maybe you're extremely kind, and make people feel good by listening and empathising. All these qualities radiate from the inside out and make you more beautiful. If your confidence is on the floor, it might help to write down all your positive traits. You have so much more to offer than simply your waistline, or how good your skin is, or how shiny your hair is. You are worth so much more than that. I am trying to take my own advice. Whenever my inner voice tries to tell me that I am not pretty enough, I remind myself that I am quirky, funny, thoughtful, I work hard, I care about my family and friends . . . and so much more. All of these things matter. It's not all about how I look.

I also think that being the hottest person in the room is a state of mind. You just have to believe you're hot, walk and talk like you're hot, and then everyone will think you are hot. Trust me on this! I am a big believer in energy, and you can give off certain energies with the way you carry yourself. Stand tall, hold your head up high, use your voice. Treat people with respect, and you will gain respect in return. All these things are essential for giving off an air of confidence. You know what they say: fake it until you make it.

One of the things that always knocked my confidence the most was being rejected – either by friends, or by men. I know this is a really common story. If a person doesn't want to date you, it can make you feel like you're unattractive, and it can feel terrible. But just because someone doesn't see your beauty (inside and out) doesn't mean you're not beautiful. It just means they can't see it for whatever reason. And that's their loss! Beauty is subjective, and you will find the right person: someone who sees everything you have to offer, and finds everything about you attractive. You are worthy of love and respect, no matter what you look like.

It might help to steer clear of anything that makes you feel bad about yourself. The mute button on Instagram is amazing – I would recommend using it as much as you need! Mute or delete accounts from people who look too perfect, and make you feel less-than. Instead, fill your feed with people who look like you, or who make you feel good about yourself. The great thing about the internet is there are so many accounts you can follow – there are so many different online communities. Find one that fits who you are, and who you want to be, and stay away from anything that makes you feel negative.

Of course, it's fine to want to change your looks. We can't be 100 per cent positive about the way we look, 100 per cent of the time. That's just not realistic. And it's totally OK to buy that make-up or try some different clothes, or even to care about your weight. Yes, feeling more beautiful can make you more confident. But it won't help if you aren't thinking about your internal self, too. Looking after yourself on the inside is even more important than on the outside. It's like having a birthday cake that looks amazing on the outside – covered in beautiful icing and glitter – but when you cut into it, it's all mouldy and disgusting. If you eat that, you'll get sick. If you try too hard to look beautiful, at the expense of your mental health, it could make you really unwell. Looking after your appearance should never come at the expense of your mind and soul.

I know there's a lot of pressure to look good these days – and trust me, I've been there. In the past, I have wanted to change everything about myself, and I have thrived off validation and approval. I wish I could go back and tell my younger self that she was enough, exactly as she was. But I can't – so I'll say it to you instead. You are enough, exactly as you are!

I have learned that beauty isn't the key to confidence. Yes, it can be a small piece of the puzzle. The rest of the puzzle is about knowing who you are, and staying true to what you care about and what you enjoy. Remember that the validation you feel when someone hits 'like' on your picture will wear off. True validation comes from being able to click 'like' on yourself, every single day – without the filter.

Chapter 3

YOU'LL NEVER BE AS YOUNG AS YOU ARE RIGHT NOW

When I turned eighteen years old, I couldn't wait to spread my wings and be independent for the first time. Of course, I loved my family so much, but my parents weren't exactly laid-back. They could be quite strict; they didn't like me coming home late, or hanging out with the wrong sorts of people. I know it's just because they were protective and wanted to make sure I was OK. But you can imagine how excited I was when it came time to apply to university. I saw uni as freedom and escape, doing what I wanted away from the eyes of my parents for the first time in my life.

I knew I wanted to go to university somewhere far away from home. I was desperate to start afresh with people who didn't know me, and explore a new place. Besides my adventures in pageants and trips to Turkey, I had hardly gone further than London. It had been instilled in me that studying and getting a degree was the right thing to do, and I couldn't wait to achieve a double whammy: making my parents proud, while also having the time of my life. When it came to deciding what to study at uni, my choice was easy. I was a born performer and wanted to study acting. I applied to three universities, including the University of Central Lancashire, which is in Preston. I remember travelling up for my audition, feeling so excited, listening to a Spotify playlist of all my favourite eighties songs. I looked out the window at fields of sheep and thought, *Wow, I'm in the middle of nowhere* – and I loved that. It felt far away from everything I knew. When I got to the station, I asked a member of staff for help getting to the university. I had never heard a northern accent in my life, believe it or not, and I was taken aback by how friendly they sounded! Even before I arrived at the uni, I had a big smile on my face. I knew this was where I wanted to be.

For my audition, I had to perform a Shakespeare monologue, as well as an improvisation piece with other people who were there to audition. When I was told that I had got in, I squealed with excitement. But I thought I'd play a joke on my parents first, and really put my acting skills to the test.

'I didn't make it,' I said when I called them, faking disappointment. They were swearing and saying, 'What the hell?' – and then I said, 'Ha, only joking!' Then we were all squealing together. All I could think of was how I needed to go shopping for all my house stuff. I couldn't wait to start my new life in Preston.

When my parents dropped me off at my university halls of residence, I knew I'd miss them, but I was itching to meet all my new housemates. Mum told me later that my dad burst into tears on the car ride home – I think it was hard for them to let their little girl go. I thought that was really moving, because my dad isn't the kind of person to show a lot of emotion. But they knew it was time for me to grow up and forge my own path.

As soon as I had unpacked, I went straight to knock on everyone's doors, introducing myself as 'Susie' (I didn't want people taking the piss out of me for my real name again). The *Only Way is Essex* was huge at the time, so I think people were pretty impressed that I came from Essex, even though I really wasn't that glamorous and I didn't have a particularly strong Essex accent.

People here were all from different backgrounds – it was so different to my time at high school, when most people had looked and sounded the same. People here had different styles and music tastes, yet we all chatted and welcomed each other. It was such a nice environment, and I knew I was where I was supposed to be. It was Fresher's Week, and of course, it's quite normal to get carried away. And that's exactly what happened. One of the girls I met invited me to pre-drinks in her kitchen, and there were tins of lager and cards everywhere. We played the drinking card game 'Ring of Fire', and the person who lost had to down the whole drink in the middle of the ring (which was made up of a mixture of everyone's drinks – cider, vodka, beer, wine . . . you name it. It was disgusting). I kept losing, and I remember everyone shouting 'Chug, chug, chug!' I can't really remember much after that, except knowing vaguely that we went to a club and had more shots (they were only £1 at the time – imagine!). The next morning, I woke up wearing the same clothes as the night before. Someone had pooped in the hallway (I kid you not). Someone else had puked in the kitchen sink. It was almost like the film *The Hangover* – it was utterly crazy. I had to stay in bed for two days, throwing up continuously. I'm not saying I stopped drinking completely after that, but wow – it was an early wake-up call. It also made me realise I was making decisions just to be liked – even if it meant putting myself at risk. That said, I don't regret it. I think all young people have a bit of a wild night as soon as they're away from their parents! It's basically a rite of passage.

Still, I wasn't at uni just to get wasted. I wanted to live independently, make friends and hone my acting skills. I know it sounds so simple, but I loved going to the supermarket to shop for my own food to cook myself. I'd buy bottles of cheap wine and have a glass while I cooked because it made me feel so grown up! Studying Acting was so interesting, too. I thought it was just going to be all about the acting, reading a script and being convincing on stage. But the degree was so much more than that; we had to write essays and learn about the techniques and history behind acting. I hadn't realised how much it would push me – in a good way. As the years went on, I spent a lot of nights in the library. I remember sitting there with piles of books and Red Bull cans all around me, sometimes working until 9am the next morning.

The acting side of things was also completely unexpected. We were taught a medieval acting technique designed to make you feel emotion naturally. One day, we all came into the drama studio and it was pitch black. Our teachers told us to sit on the floor and then, all of a sudden, I was slapped in the face and drenched with water. Then, they were shouting at all of us: 'How do you feel? Are you angry? Are you sad? Let out all the traumas of your past!' I was so hungover that day that all I wanted to do was sleep. But it was so intense, and soon I found myself bursting into tears, rocking back and forth, repeating, 'You're OK, you're OK.' In the end, it was an awakening experience I'll never forget! I think it made me a better actor – more in touch with my raw emotions.

I also became part of a group of girlfriends for the first time in my life. By the time uni rolled around, I had drifted a bit from Lucy. People grow and change, and you won't stay close to the same people for ever – and that's totally OK. There's nothing wrong with making new friends to suit the person you are now. I met my three uni girls one night at the student union. They started out as 'night-out friends' – just girls who had lots of fun together – but became actual, supportive, ride-or-die friends. I knew they'd be important people in my life when, on a whim, I invited them to one of my performances. I said, 'If you can make it, that would be great, but no pressure!' I honestly didn't think they'd show up. But they came to my show with a bottle of wine and flowers. I felt so cared for and loved thanks to that little gesture. I remember I kept the wine on my bookshelf in my room and didn't drink it for ages; I looked at it to remind myself that people did actually love and care for me. As someone who had struggled with friendships and feeling accepted her whole life, it really felt so important.

They were good friends to me, and I tried to be a good friend to them as well. They were all really clever, successful and strong, which positively influenced me, but they also had their own insecurities and boy troubles that I tried to help them through. Like all the best friendships, it was really about give and take. We'd listen to each other and be there with cups of tea or glasses of wine whenever the shit hit the fan. Encouraging them made me feel really good. I felt like I was part of something, and that was a huge turning point. It made me feel much more confident, and gave me a sense of belonging.

Adventures in Love and Heartbreak

Those friendships meant the world to me when I went through my first break-up. When I arrived at university, I was still a virgin, which took a lot of people by surprise. But you'll know by now that I stick to what I believe in and I follow my heart, and I really wanted to have an emotional connection with the first person I had sex with. I had kissed a few boys in college while studying for my BTEC, but it had never really gone any further, and I was fine with that. I hadn't met the right person.

That is, until I met my first boyfriend – let's call him 'Boyfriend 1' – on a night out. Maybe it was the beer goggles, but when he walked into the club, I genuinely thought he was Prince Charming. It felt like time stopped when I saw him, and nothing else mattered. All I wanted was to speak to him and get to know him. Thankfully, I caught his eye too – and he came over to buy me a drink. We started chatting, and I could immediately feel the chemistry; it was like nothing I had experienced before. We exchanged numbers and started texting and going on dates to bars and cheap restaurants. After a few weeks, we became boyfriend and girlfriend, and a few weeks later, we had sex for the first time. I waited until I was sure he wanted me for me, and not just to have sex. I'm so glad I did. Of course, there's nothing wrong with sleeping with someone earlier on – I just did what was right for me, and I'm proud of myself for not giving in to peer pressure. You'll be pressured to do all sorts of things throughout your life, and it's important to remember that the people who put pressure on you will come and go – but you'll always have yourself. So, always make decisions according to what *you* want, and learn to block out everyone else's opinions.

Boyfriend 1 was my first proper relationship, and we were together for about a year. I met his family, and he came down to Essex to meet mine (although my parents didn't let us sleep in the same room). I honestly thought I was going to be with this boy for ever – I was so blinded by my infatuation. But I don't think he had the same idea, which I guess is to be expected. We were only nineteen years old; we still had our whole lives ahead of us. He didn't really take the relationship as seriously as I did. He would go out with his boys all the time and get black-out drunk, and I'd get upset that I didn't know where he was. And then one night, I spotted him on the other side of a club, kissing another girl, right in front of me. I felt absolutely broken. I grabbed my friends and they took me home; I sobbed the whole way. The next day, I confronted him, and he said he'd been so drunk that he didn't remember it. He didn't think it was that big a deal – but I knew it was over. I just felt so betrayed and humiliated, and didn't understand how he could do that to me.

You never forget your first heartbreak, and ending things with Boyfriend 1 really did hit me like a ton of bricks. I cried to my friends and family on the phone every day for weeks, and I found it hard to focus on my uni work. It felt like the end of the world – I thought I'd never get over him. But time is the greatest healer, and ultimately I know that this experience made me stronger. I was lucky to have so much amazing support around me. My uni girls suggested we go on holiday to Spain to take my mind off things. We went to Marbella, and it was my first time going away with friends. I had been working behind the bar in one of the local clubs at uni, so I saved some money to pay for my own flights and hotel, and it was just the tonic I needed. Sun, sand and my best mates. We drank and laughed, and I think I only cried once. They really helped me get over this guy, and I'm so grateful.

But it wasn't just the holiday to Spain that helped me move on. My break-up helped me realise that I couldn't necessarily rely on other people for my happiness, because people don't always treat you in the way you hope to be treated. This was a key lesson in why it's so important to look after yourself and work out what makes you happy. Sure, the support I received from other people was huge – but I also had to learn to love myself. I decided to write a list of things I liked doing, and made it my mission to tick one off every day: things like baking cupcakes, singing loudly in the shower, going to the gym. Every time I did something for me, it took my mind off my ex. I wasn't thinking of him; I was thinking of me.

And that made me love myself more and more. I highly recommend writing your own list of things that make you happy, and work on doing at least one every day. It might help you invest more energy into your most important relationship: the one you have with yourself.

A few months later, I felt like I was fully over him. And it was at this point that he texted me and tried to get me back one more time (I'm sure a lot of you will relate to this . . .).

'Hey, how are you? It would be nice to see you xx,' read the text on my phone.

And I completely ignored it.

If it wasn't for the sense of betrayal I'd felt, and all the effort I'd put into working on myself since, I don't think I would have had the strength to do that. But I felt strong enough to know better – I wasn't going to go down that path again. To this day, that was probably the most intense relationship I've ever had. I think it's normal for your first experience of love to be almost obsessive. I don't necessarily think that's healthy, but I do think these experiences of heartbreak make us who we are, and we take these lessons with us into our future relationships. It's all part of growing up, and heartbreak actually makes your heart grow bigger.

It also meant I knew the important qualities to look for when going into my second relationship. When I was in my third year of university, I met Boyfriend 2 online. He was eight years older than me and worked as a lawyer in London. On our first date, we had such interesting conversations, and I loved the fact he had his own life and income – he was so much more mature than the guys at my uni. We carried on dating, and eventually he became my boyfriend. I credit him with so much of my growth during my early twenties. He was so intelligent, and we'd watch documentaries together and talk about the law and other things that mattered. He also loved fitness, so we'd go to the gym and train together. This was when I learned how thrilling it is to become physically stronger, because it makes you feel emotionally stronger too. He was so hardworking and he inspired me to work hard, too. He would help me rehearse my lines for whatever play I was working on, and he wouldn't stop until I felt like I had got it right. Then, he'd travel all the way up to Preston to watch my performances. He even came to my graduation when my parents couldn't make it. He cried when I walked on to the stage in my cap and gown. It was so nice feeling loved like that.

It definitely wasn't a perfect relationship – of course, we fought. I'd put my foot down if I wasn't happy about something, and he would do the same. But we'd work through it and apologise if we needed to. Boyfriend 2 really cared for me, and he made me a better version of myself. I loved who I was when I was with him – confident and interested in the world. Once I'd graduated, he helped me get my first job in London, and we carried on dating while I lived at home with my parents in Essex. But eventually, our age difference became too noticeable; he was ready to settle down, while I was only just getting started in the world. I wanted adventures and new experiences. I knew I wouldn't have my youth again – and he knew that, too – so our relationship ended amicably. We stayed in touch for a few years after our break-up; he was still someone I trusted unconditionally and felt I could rely on. But sometimes, it's just not meant to be. I will always be extremely grateful for having had him in my life, though. I think he taught me what a mature, loving relationship should look like. It should always be about bringing out the best in the other person, and supporting each other no matter what. I'm not saying I always got it right after him (as we will see in Chapter 5), but I'm glad I had that framework for what a good relationship actually is.

Highs, Lows and Lessons Learned

A huge part of growing up is going through difficult times. You can't skip the hard times, because they make you who you are, and you learn as you go. I discovered this when I moved to London for my first job post-uni. I knew in my heart that I wanted to pursue acting, but I also knew that head shots and travelling to auditions could be expensive, and I didn't want to work in a bar or a café to make ends meet. So Boyfriend 2 encouraged me to apply for a job in finance, starting out in an admin role. Your first proper job is always a learning curve, let me tell you! I had difficult colleagues and had to prove myself again and again. It could be hard, but it was also an incredible opportunity for growth.

Getting up every day and putting on my smart clothes for my City job made me feel like the main character in a movie, and I always think it's important to absorb the attitudes of people around you. I was the youngest person in my company, but I watched the powerful businesswomen around me and observed how they showed their strength. They all had brilliant posture and tones of voice, and I remember thinking: *Wow, they know what they're doing.* I wanted to be like that! Eventually, they realised that I was eager to learn and I earned their trust, and I'd spend my Friday nights out with people my granddad's age talking about tax returns. As I've said, I've always enjoyed being around older people. I think the conversations can be more striking and interesting, especially when those people have been through a lot in their lives. I would encourage everyone to get to know older people – you may just learn a thing or two.

It was during this time, though, that I experienced one of the scarier incidents in my life. After my relationship with Boyfriend 2 ended, I went on a date with another man. I wasn't really ready to be in another relationship, but it was just a bit of fun. On our date, something weird happened: I lost my phone. Obviously, I was panicking, but the guy said he would buy me a new one. It seemed like quite an excessive gesture, but he seemed to have money (he'd dropped me home in a Lamborghini) and I was stressed about my phone, so I accepted. A couple of days later, he showed up at my house with a new phone, but he gave it to me unboxed. I probably should've realised that was a red flag, but I was naive and trusting at the time. I started using the phone, while still talking to this man occasionally.

A few weeks later, I received a really scary email. 'I know everything about you. I've been studying you very closely for the past few months,' the email read. I thought it must've been some kind of joke or spam, but then I clicked the picture attached to the email and it was a picture I had sent to my ex of me in a bra and shorts. Then, more messages started coming: this person was telling me they had lots of information about me, and they planned to ruin all my relationships. Frantically, I called my ex. He was the only person I felt like I could rely on for something like this. He thought this man had probably stolen my old phone on our date, and put some kind of tracking device on the new phone he'd given me, which meant he could see what I was doing. I stopped using the new phone, and my ex came with me to the police to report it and hand in the phone as evidence.

Sadly, the stalker (as I called him) already had far too much information by that point, and sent troubling emails to my workplace, and even my ex's workplace. It got really out of hand, and I was scared about how much he knew and what he would do next. But I changed all my email accounts and phone numbers, and eventually the harassment stopped. I'm not exactly sure what happened to that man, but I know that a couple of months later, he came up on my friend's dating app under a completely different name. Clearly, he was a compulsive liar. I still don't understand what he wanted from me, as he never asked for money. Maybe he wanted me to lean on him and get closer to him while these scary messages came in.

To this day, I still don't understand what his intentions were, and I don't know if it would have developed into anything worse. But it was a really scary experience that made me feel paranoid, and like the world was a dangerous place. Now, I'm not quite as trusting any more if people seem to be doing good deeds. I find myself wondering, what are their motives? Could there be something more sinister going on? Just like the betrayal I'd experienced from Boyfriend 1, it showed me that people can't always be trusted. It's a harsh realisation, but it's also a useful one. It's good to be optimistic and to trust people instinctively; I am glad I am that sort of positive person. But it also pays to keep your wits about you, and to trust your gut if something seems a bit off. Your safety is so important, so if you sense something isn't right, confide in someone you trust and ask for help.

The World is Big – Embrace It!

While I was living in London and earning money for the first time, I knew I wanted to use that money to expand my horizons. And that meant travelling! I had caught a bit of a travel bug when I went to South Korea for the Miss Asia Pacific pageant – I had loved the experience of being somewhere completely different. It was just magical. So, when I'd saved up enough money, I booked a flight to go to Thailand for a month by myself.

Someone had told me that you can 'find yourself' in Thailand, and I believed them. I'm not really sure what they meant by 'find yourself', but that sounded appealing to me, as someone who always wanted to grow and improve. I also wanted to go somewhere really far away, hot, somewhat spiritual, and – most importantly – cheap. I wanted to meet people from all over the world who were there for the same reasons as me. Thailand seemed like the perfect place.

My first stop was the beautiful island of Koh Samui. There were beautiful sandy beaches, and the water was so blue, I almost didn't believe it was real. I checked myself into my first accommodation: a series of huts, almost like a camping site, near the beach. I had my own room, but I met tons of interesting people there from all over the world. They were from Australia, New Zealand and America . . . I was the only British person there, and I loved that. I'm always so intrigued to meet people from different walks of life, so I chatted to everyone and made plenty of friends.

On the third day I was there, I decided I wanted to explore the beach at night. All my new friends were tired and hungover, but I wanted to get out of my comfort zone and do something by myself. The night was eerie yet romantic, and as I wandered along the beach, it felt like the moon was guiding me towards a specific point. It's hard to explain, but it felt like a dream. I could hear the waves gently lapping the shore, their sound so soothing, and the moon was reflecting on the ocean, making it shimmer. Soon, I noticed this little beach hut with colourful beanbags outside, next to tables covered with candles and flowers. There were a few groups of people chilling and having drinks. I thought, *Wow, what an amazing opportunity to take in this incredible scenery*. So, I decided to get myself a drink and sit on one of the beanbags. The guy behind the bar didn't speak a word of English, but I somehow managed to order a mojito.

As I sat there drinking my mojito, looking out at the dark water, I felt extremely relaxed – so relaxed that I sank into my seat. And, before I knew it, the moon fell into the sea. I couldn't believe my eyes. I got up and started shouting, 'Did you see that?! The moon just shrank and fell into the sea!'

Everyone was laughing, and then I was laughing too. Everything around me seemed to change shape and colour, and I found everything anyone said completely hysterical.

'Why is everything so special?' I said to someone nearby.

'This is a mushroom bar. All the drinks are magic-mushroom shakes – and you've had a mojito, which is the strongest one!'

At first, I panicked – I had never taken illegal drugs, and certainly not a psychedelic like this. I wouldn't have ordered a drink there if I had known, but I can't deny that it was an interesting experience.

In the end, I travelled around Koh Samui, Koh Phangan, Koh Tao and Bangkok for a month, and it was incredible – even if I did get sick after eating a scorpion at one point. A lot of my friends were saying they envied me, and praised me for being brave. But I really think life begins outside your comfort zone. If you want to travel somewhere and no one else wants to go with you, just go anyway! Don't let your life be dictated by other people. And if you have the money, instead of wasting it on silly things, save it for giving yourself experiences and making unforgettable memories. These kinds of moments are worth far more than any lipstick or handbag. And you might as well do it while you're young, when you have the energy and the time. Of course, you can make amazing memories at any time of life, but it can be harder when we have more responsibilities, so make the most of your youth. Seek adventure and trust that you can make friends and look after yourself if you need to. Experiences like this can help you fall even more deeply in love with yourself.

Enjoy the Journey

When you're young, I think there's a tendency to wish your life away. I spent so much of my teens and twenties wanting to be older. There was always a big hurry. I wanted to achieve things and make something of my life. But why the big rush? When it comes down to it, you'll be old and grey, looking back on your life, and you'll want to go back. Maybe you'll want to do things differently – because maybe you spent so much time focusing on your work and goals that you forgot to enjoy yourself. Or perhaps you'll just want to relive all those amazing experiences you had. Whatever way you look at it, you just have to enjoy the current moment. You will never get these minutes and seconds back. Time is very precious, and it is what we make of it, and what we choose to do with it. I'm not saying you shouldn't have goals and ambitions (I definitely did, and I'll go into that more in the next chapter); I'm just saying you shouldn't get so worried about what's around the corner that you forget to enjoy the here and now.

My biggest piece of advice is to stop overthinking. I know that can be easier said than done, but just remind yourself that the future hasn't happened yet. And no matter how much planning you do, you'll never truly know what the future has in store for you. There's an old saying, 'Make plans, God laughs,' and I think it's so true. So much of life is beyond your control – and it's full of 'sliding door' moments. Yes, life is about working hard and making good decisions, but it's also about luck and chance. It's about meeting the right people at the right time, and in the right place – people who can change the course of your life for ever. I know that has certainly happened to me. So it helps to just stop trying to control everything all the time. You might choose one road, and then it'll collapse, and you'll have to choose another road. And that's OK. We all change, and we're all making it up as we go along.

The truth is, you might think you know everything when you're eighteen and you're flying the nest for the first time, ready to start your life. But in reality, you won't really know who you are until you're much older. I'd say I have a pretty good grasp of who I am now, but I also know that nothing is definite. I am still always learning, growing and evolving. You never hit a point where you're like, 'OK, I'm an adult. I'm all grown up now!' You can go through all the motions of being an adult – paying bills, even having children and getting married – but you'll still be a kid deep down, and you'll still shift and change in ways you aren't even aware of yet. It's pretty exciting when you think about it.

I know I made some mistakes as I went through my late teens and early twenties, but I wouldn't take any of them back, because they have all led me to where I am today. Our mistakes and hard times help us learn, and they make us better. You won't ever 'complete' life, and that's the beauty of it. The older I get, the more I'm loving it. Because I keep gaining more knowledge, and growing the relationship I have with myself. I might not be that wide-eyed girl who went off to uni any more, but I'm still young, and I plan to embrace everything life has in store – the good, the bad and the ugly too.

Chapter 4

KEEP HOLD OF YOUR DREAMS – AND THE REST WILL FOLLOW

The whole time I was working in London, my dream of being an actor stayed front and centre in my mind. I just loved everything about acting. To me, it felt like a way of escaping the world I was in and getting into other people's worlds and minds instead. I loved studying characters who were very different to me – like a fifty-year-old woman with several kids – and working out how they think, how they talk, how they walk, and what made them who they are. To be an actor, you have to be able to be like playdough and mould yourself into lots of different things. I have always felt a lot of pressure in my life to be 'normal' and acting removed that pressure – because I didn't have to fit into one specific mould. In a way, we are all actors, playing different roles in different parts of our lives. As Shakespeare said, 'All the world's a stage.'

Being on stage was such a high – it felt like euphoria, or falling in love. It might sound weird, but I've always had a romantic connection with the stage. Imagining myself on stage would fill my heart up. I loved everything about it: the energy, the smell, the lights, the way my voice echoed, the way I could hardly see the audience, but still knew they were there. It was just everything to me.

In addition to my day job, I had signed with an acting agency based in Manchester, and they would occasionally get me auditions. Whenever I had one, I had to lie to work and pretend I was ill, when actually I was in Covent Garden auditioning for a Coca-Cola advert. It was really hard to keep this up – that's why a lot of actors work in flexible jobs like bars, cafés and fitness training – but I felt like I needed the money from my finance job for my acting profile shoots and showreels. It was so hard keeping both going at the same time – I felt like I had one foot out the door at my job, but I also didn't have enough time to commit to my acting. In the end, I knew I needed to make a change. Not long after I returned from Thailand, I decided to quit my job to follow my dreams. I didn't know how I was going to do it, but I had a feeling my time was going to come.

Auditioning in the UK had been getting me down, so I wanted to take a break from it all. I packed my bags and booked a one-way ticket to Istanbul, the biggest city in Turkey, my motherland. I didn't really have any expectations about going there – I thought maybe I'd explore and then come back after a few weeks. I arrived in Istanbul with basically no plans, just the address of the hostel where I planned to stay. When I arrived, I couldn't find it for the life of me, and I had to phone my dad to help me navigate there! It turned out the hostel looked nothing like the pictures – it was grimy and horrible – so after a few days, a friend introduced me to an older lady she knew who had a spare room. She told me I could stay as long as I needed for a cheap rent. This worked out well for me, as my savings were already running low. I know people think actors live extremely glamorous lives – and, of course, the very successful ones do – but I always remembered my uni tutor telling us that very few people make money from acting. You need to be prepared to be poor, and to do it because it's your passion, not because you hope it'll make you rich and famous. Of course, I had my ambitions, but I knew that the financial struggle is just part of an actor's life – and I was willing to do it.

Istanbul was a real culture shock for me. When I used to go to Turkey as a kid, I had mostly spent time in the countryside with my grandparents and cousins. Istanbul was extremely busy, and I can distinctly remember the smell of cars and petrol. I also quickly realised my Turkish wasn't as good as I thought it was. Everywhere I went, I was perceived as a tourist because of my English accent. It's weird that, at first, I felt like an outsider in my own country – especially because, back in the UK, I'd felt like an outsider because I was Turkish. I could never really win.

It's crazy how your life can change just from being in the right place at the right time. This is why I always say to go to that party, get out there in the world – because you never know who you might meet, and who might give you the opportunity you're looking for. And that's exactly what happened to me.

I went to see a play with the woman I was living with. I went along because I wanted to see what kinds of acting opportunities there might be for me here, hoping that maybe I would have better luck here than in the UK. The play was good, but it was what happened during the interval that made the night really special. I spotted a man called Müjdat Gezen, who is a famous and well-respected producer in Turkey. I remembered my dad had spoken about him before – like me, my dad loved acting when he was young, and this man was his idol. Straight away, I messaged my dad. 'Go and speak to him!' my dad encouraged me. So, with his confidence instilled in me, I strutted over to him to introduce myself.

I told him how much I respected his work, and that my name was Ekin-Su and I was an actor from the UK. He was lovely, and within five minutes, he had said: 'Come and see me next week. Let's have a chat. I like your energy – you're very unique.' He gave me his business card, and we set up a meeting for the following week. I couldn't believe my luck at seeing him there that day, but I'm also glad I was bold enough to go and introduce myself.

The next week, I went for a meeting with him and we chatted about my goals, and he told me about some upcoming projects he was working on. I told him I would love to act in a Turkish soap, and he said he could get me a role in one. He also said that I should stay in Turkey for six months and try to pursue acting here – he thought my Englishness was unique and that I could do really well. I'm so grateful for him for believing in me – and within a couple of weeks, I had my first role in a soap! I was so excited to be being paid for my acting, let alone on TV. I had only ever done plays before, so it felt like a massive progression. I had a very small role as a doctor in an episode of a soap called *Back Streets*, which was set in a hospital (a bit like *Casualty* in the UK) and aired every Saturday.

My first time being on set was so overwhelming and exciting. I loved the buzzy atmosphere – there were about sixty to seventy people on set, and I had the most amazing hair and make-up that transformed me from Ekin-Su into this well-respected doctor. When I was filming the scene, they did so many takes. I had to say my lines around five times, while the cameramen got different shots of my reactions to what the other person was saying, and captured different angles. I was shocked by how much detail went into it. Looking back now, it was the worst acting I had ever done – but it was such a great stepping stone. I was one step closer to living the dream!

Ekin-Su, the Popstar

As the months went by, I was settling more into my life in Istanbul. That producer sponsored me to receive Turkish lessons, so my accent was really improving, which meant I felt more like I was fitting in. He also gave me a few small roles in his plays, and I absolutely loved getting up on stage. I was also starting to make new friends, both within the industry and outside it.

One night, I was invited to a party by one of the producers I had worked with. Everyone was having fun, and people were taking it in turns to sing songs on a little stage. Of course, I'll never pass up an opportunity to get on stage, so I grabbed the microphone and started singing 'I Will Always Love You' by Whitney Houston – one of my all-time favourites. I didn't realise it at the time, but there was a guy there from a record company, and he recorded me singing on his Instagram story. Five minutes later, that man pulled me to the side to show me the video. 'My boss at Sony Music just messaged me asking who you are,' he said. Again, it was one of those moments that was a mixture of luck and boldness – and then he said: 'How would you feel about recording a single?'

I was shocked. I have always loved singing, but it was never my primary passion, and I didn't think I was good enough to make it as a singer. At first, I thought he was joking, but he gave me his card and I looked him up online – it was completely legit. I didn't have high expectations, but I thought, *Screw it, why not? It could be fun.*

A week and a half later, the man was introducing me to another Turkish singer, who he wanted me to work with on this single he was recording. The plan was to cover a popular Turkish song that had been a hit in the 1980s, but to bring it in to the modern day, making it girly and empowering. Next thing I knew, I was in the recording studio, bringing the single to life! It was like a dream, and I was so happy to be there. Just as I had been in the TV studio, I was surprised by the attention to detail and how many takes we'd do. One of the music producers would ask me to repeat my lines with more emotion, and I'd record lines in different pitches so they could all be blended together. I had been a bit self-conscious about my voice, as I didn't think I was the best singer in the world. But one of the producers explained that it's not all about having the best voice – it's about your charisma and your presence. You can hone your voice with work and practice, but it's actually harder to engage with the audience and perform. I knew performing was in my bones, so I took her words on board and let that confidence carry me through.

Not long after recording the song, it was time to film the music video! It was so much fun. The other singer and I had so much fun looking through the rails of outfits, and going through each shot of the music video. There was one scene where we were in a car with smoke coming out of it. The director gave instructions like: 'Reach out to the camera! Give me everything!' It was hilarious, and I was grinning from ear to ear. We did so many takes for a three-minute song – it took hours. But it was one of the best experiences ever.

The next stage in the single's release was going around Turkey and Cyprus to perform it! At this point, I really felt like a proper superstar. I loved performing on stage and hearing the crowds sing every word. The record label would pay for everything and treat me like a queen. I had my own personal trainer and bodyguard.

The song did really well, but eventually the hype started to die down, as it always does. And when the gigs stopped, I realised that I needed to make a choice – I could continue down this path as a singer and try to get another hit single, or I could go back to my dream of being an actor. I knew that it would be too hard to give my all to both, so I decided to get back to acting. I think many of us have these moments in life where we're at a crossroads, and we don't know which path to take. But all I can say is follow your gut, and then make peace with whatever decision you make. Whatever happens, you'll make the best of it. Stay committed, and you'll get where you want to go.

Making it Happen

Once I had decided to get back into acting, I reached out to the famous producer to see if he had any opportunities for me. He gave me a role in his newest play – a bigger role this time. It was a comedy, and I was playing a housewife in the 1960s. The theatre was huge, almost like the Royal Albert Hall. Rehearsing and performing every night was an amazing experience, and I was so glad I had chosen to go back to acting. It was where my heart was, and I still had big dreams to play a villain or a detective. Sometimes I want to go back there and remember who I used to be.

In acting, you often get offered your next role because an agent or casting director comes to see you in whatever you're working on now. This is what happened for me. Someone from ATV, one of the most popular TV channels in Turkey, came to see me perform and thought I'd be perfect for a role in a new soap they were making. The role was for an English tourist, and the character would need to be attractive, quirky, funny and flirty. I thought, *Oh my god, this role is made for me!* So I met the director and, amazingly, he agreed. When I found out I had got the job – my first leading, permanent role in a soap – I could hardly believe it. I jumped for joy and called my parents, who were so proud of me.

Within weeks, I was moving to the mountains – about an eight-hour drive away – to live with my co-stars in a hotel near the set. I packed my bags and said goodbye to the lady I had lived with, from whom I had learned so much. She had supported me through all my random Turkish adventures and saying goodbye was bittersweet, but I couldn't believe I was now entering into the next stage of my life as a proper soap actor.

The episodes were filmed weekly, and there was a lot of pressure to learn lines before every scene. Sometimes, we'd be given our lines and told we needed to learn them by lunchtime the next day. It was challenging, but exhilarating. You had to be on the ball constantly – nobody wanted to be the person who held up filming because they didn't know what they were doing. Sometimes, I felt intimidated – especially being around other actors who had more experience than me. I'd feel embarrassed if I forgot my lines, and sometimes I'd feel paranoid and worry that I wasn't good enough. I had to remind myself that everyone starts somewhere, and that I was still learning. Thankfully, all the staff and my co-stars were so encouraging, and my confidence grew much more as time went on.

Every week, after the show had been broadcast, we'd find out how well the episode had done – basically, how many people were tuning in. There was a lot of focus on the ratings. When an episode did well, it would give us all a massive boost of motivation going into the next episode. It was so exciting that so many people were watching us and enjoying the show. I started to become more well known. When I was back in Istanbul (I could now afford my own place there) or walking around the local town, I'd occasionally get recognised. It was so exciting, and a little taster of what was to come later on.

I'd say this was one of the happiest times in my life. I was doing what I loved and making friends, and I felt respected and acknowledged for something I was truly passionate about. I felt like I was really finding and understanding myself, and learning to love myself even more. I was working hard and being rewarded for it. At the same time, it wasn't all rainbows and butterflies. I was in my first toxic relationship (which I'll explain more in the next chapter), and I also knew that there were dark things happening behind the scenes in the acting industry. There were some producers in the industry who could be seedy and try it on with the female actors. Luckily I didn't have any bad experiences, but I did witness it happening. It just shows that even behind the dream life, nothing is ever perfect. You always have to look out for yourself, and remember not to be too naive and trusting.

After a year of working on the soap, filming stopped when the pandemic happened. Like everyone else, I found it extremely hard to suddenly be locked down in my Istanbul flat. I knew I had a choice: I could either go stir crazy, eat my entire body weight in food and drink gallons of wine, or I could try and improve myself, read a lot of books, work on my mental health and practise my acting. I went with the second option, and really tried to make the best of it. When filming started up again, I was motivated and excited to be back at work. And it was during this time that another opportunity would come my way – probably the biggest one of my life to date. But more on that later . . .

Never Give Up On Your Dreams

I know my story so far might make it sound like I had it easy. I had a lot of lucky breaks, and moments where things seemed to fall into place for me. But there were also so many hiccups along the way, and so many people who doubted my journey, and whether I would ever make it. People had told me, 'You'll never get a job in acting' and 'acting is a waste of time'. I had struggled to get anywhere with my acting while I was living in London, and it just shows that sometimes you need to make a change and try something different to get on to the path you were destined to be on. Just because your dreams don't come true straight away, doesn't mean they won't come true at all. It might just mean you need to switch it up and try something new.

When you experience setbacks, it's so easy to just give up, especially when you have people around you who don't necessarily believe in you. My parents and my brother always supported me, but I had other relatives who laughed at me when I said I wanted to be an actress, and told me I should pursue a 'proper career' because I was never going to make it. But I never listened to them. In fact, it just made me more determined. If someone said I wasn't good enough, I'd think: *Fuck you, I'm going to prove you wrong*. It would push me even harder, and motivate me even more. I think the hardest-working, most successful people are the ones who had people telling them they wouldn't become anything. It lights a fire inside you and makes you even stronger.

Of course, it's hard dealing with rejection and failure. It happens a lot in acting, but it also happens in every career. You have to grow a thick skin. There will always be people who don't see your potential, or who won't take a chance on you. But all you can do is keep trying and keep being yourself, and I promise that someone eventually will. It's all about putting yourself out there, and giving yourself the opportunity to be lucky. All it takes is one person, or one moment, and then everything can fall into place. You don't need everything to go right for you – you just need one thing to go right, and then you can watch the dominoes fall.

When you do get hit by setbacks, it can feel like a punch in the gut. Trust me, I've been there. I know the feeling of getting a call after an audition that I had spent days preparing for and being told I hadn't made it through. I know it's a cliché but I do believe that when one door closes, another one opens. And it also helps to remember that everything is temporary. It can feel like the end of the world if you don't get the job you want, or if you get rejected from your dream uni. But I promise that feeling won't last. Remember that whenever it rains, sunshine is just around the corner. You might even see a rainbow. It's normal to feel like something is the end of the world – allow yourself to mourn whatever it is you wanted. But talk to your friends, do something you love, and remember that life works in unexpected ways, and good things are coming. It's all about being a positive person, viewing the glass as half full instead of half empty. The happiest people in life aren't the ones who never have setbacks – they're the ones who can look at setbacks in a positive light, and believe that everything happens for a reason. It might seem like this comes naturally to me, but I have to remind myself to think positively every day.

You might have heard of 'the law of attraction'. It's the idea that if you put positive thoughts out into the world, positive things will come back to you. I do believe there's something to be said for this. It's not so much that something magic happens, it's more that you become more open to opportunities. I always held on to the positive idea that I would make it as an actor. So I went to those plays, I put myself in the right place to meet that producer, and things started to fall into place. 'Manifesting' isn't just willing something into existence and waiting for it to fall into your lap – it's all about putting those positive beliefs into action. It's about keeping your dreams front and centre in your mind, even when you get knocked back.

I really recommend reading some books that will motivate you and inspire you. You're already reading this one, but I also recommend *The Power of Now* by Eckhart Tolle, *F**k it: The Ultimate Spiritual Way* by John C. Parkin and *Manifest* by Roxie Nafousi. Whatever it is you're dreaming of, throw yourself into that topic. Listen to podcasts, read articles from people who are doing what you long to do, and work out how they got there. Maybe even reach out and ask someone to meet you for a coffee and share some advice. You never know where these connections will lead. The more proactive you are, the greater the chance your dreams will come true.

I've always been told I'm a daydreamer. Even at school, I would get told off for gazing out of the window. I was always imagining how my life might turn out, and always tried to will it into reality. I have always wanted the best of everything. It's the opposite of logic, but I truly believe it has got me to where I am today. I'm not very good at being told 'no', or accepting that something won't work. I am always in 'la-la land', being completely unrealistic with outlandish ideas. I think we all have this capacity for self-belief deep down, but for some of us, it gets dragged out of us when we're constantly told 'no'. Think about that amazing imagination you had when you were a kid, and go back there. There's nothing wrong with believing in yourself.

You have to keep hold of your dreams and protect them at all costs. You have to believe that they are valid and achievable. You have to trust your intuition, trust the signs in your life that seem to tell you which way to go. Of course, we rely on other people to do well in life. We need people to believe in us, to help get us where we want to go. But no one will believe in you if you don't believe in yourself. You have more control over your life than you think you do. YOU have the power to make your dreams come true.

It's also important to let your dreams shift and change. Be open to what life throws at you. If you're reading this book, you'll probably know that my big break didn't actually turn out to be acting. Instead, I ended up winning the UK's biggest reality TV show. You can make all the plans in the world, but life won't always follow them – and sometimes that's for the best. Maybe something even bigger and better is waiting for you.

Chapter 5

NEVER LET TOXIC RELATIONSHIPS DIM YOUR GLOW

I think all of us grow up with a fairy tale about what love should look like. If you're a similar age to me, you would've grown up with Disney stories, watching princesses being saved by handsome, romantic princes, and living happily ever after. And then, when you hit your teenage years, you would've loved romcoms, which are basically just fairy tales for grown-ups. They're amazing, and I still love them, but they do give you unrealistic ideas about what love will be like.

My favourite romcom was *13 Going On 30*, which is about a girl who gets transported through time to her glamorous thirty-year-old life, and (spoiler) realises that the love of her life is actually her geeky best friend from school (who ends up being hot, of course). I really resonated with Jennifer Garner's character, Jenna. I was also picked on at school, and dreamed of creating a beautiful life away from the people who bullied me. In some ways, I've manifested that film, because I am truly living my dreams now. But that movie also gave me an idea of the perfect relationship, setting the bar very high. I always wanted to meet someone like Matt (played by Mark Ruffalo). I wanted the guy who could be my best friend, with good morals and a good career, and someone I could be silly around.

But as you grow up, you realise that the stories portrayed in romantic films aren't realistic – or that they're only possible for the very lucky few. When I was twenty-one, my parents got divorced, so I was beginning to realise that love doesn't always work out the way you hope it will. Most people don't live those kinds of fairy tales, and they aren't lucky enough to meet their perfect person who will always love and care for them, no matter what. Not straight away, anyway. Unfortunately, I learned that the hard way throughout my twenties.

I've already spoken about my early experiences with boys. My crushes were a big reason why I became the Ekin-Su I am today. But, like most teenagers, my earliest romantic experinces were pretty awkward.

I had my first kiss when I was about thirteen years old, while I was on holiday in Turkey. We always stayed at my grandparents' house; I had loads of friends there and we'd all go to the beach together. One day, I noticed this boy kept making eye contact with me at the beach, and it gave me butterflies. I'm not sure if I even fancied him or just enjoyed the attention, but it was exciting. I wasn't used to having a member of the opposite sex pay attention to me like this. I was embarrassed and looked away, but I couldn't stop thinking about it.

I saw him again when I went with my friends to the neighbourhood park later in the evening. He came over to me and asked if I'd like to go for a walk. Giddily, I agreed – not even realising what the time was and forgetting my parents were expecting me home at 11pm. We walked around the summer villas, and even though our chat was really awkward (him telling me about his favourite music, and me trying to keep up in broken Turkish), it felt so romantic walking through the streets with this boy, with the stars sparkling overhead. Eventually, we made it back to the beach, where there was live music playing. I sat down with the boy, and he leaned in to kiss me. I didn't know anything about kissing except what I'd seen in the movies, so I think I just opened my mouth and breathalysed him. He didn't know what he was doing, either – it was like both mouths meeting for ten seconds, with our eyes wide open looking at each other. Suddenly, the earlier romance was gone – I hated it. I thought, *If this is what kissing is, why do people like doing it?!*

Anyway, I didn't have to do it for too much longer, because I was saved (and mortified) by my dad angrily shouting 'Ekin-Su!!!!' from across the beach. It was 1am by that point, so he'd come out looking for me. He dragged me home with him, and I never spoke to that boy again. What an embarrassing experience.

But I think that's the defining word for romance when you're young: embarrassment. And if you didn't have embarrassing experiences, then I think you're very lucky. Looking back over my teenage years, my interactions with boys (and sometimes men) could be uncomfortable. It seems to be changing more now, but when I was younger, there was definitely a culture of men making you feel like you were a piece of meat. It happened all the time.

I remember chatting on MSN Messenger to boys at school, and being asked to flash my bra. The first thing they'd say was, 'Go on, show us your boobs!' If you didn't, they'd bully you. If you did, that was a good thing – but then you were also at risk of being called a 'slut'. The girls could basically never win.

It was this mindset that led me into my first two relationships, which I've already spoken about in Chapter 3. To recap: there was Boyfriend 1, who I genuinely thought was Prince Charming, but turned out to be immature and cheated on me right in front of my face. And then there was Boyfriend 2, who was actually the blueprint of what a good relationship is. He was kind and supportive, and I believe our time together made me into a better person, but the age difference ended up being too hard, and so we went our separate ways. I don't regret either of these relationships, because they taught me useful lessons and helped me become the woman I am now. But when I got to Turkey, I had a couple of relationships I probably would've preferred not to have happened at all, because they were so toxic and left permanent scars. I'm sharing my story here in the hope that it might help you to avoid the same mistakes.

It Always Begins Well . . .

I met my first Turkish boyfriend while I was still living in Istanbul, during my singing career. Let's call him Adam. We met at a bar and ended up chatting all night. He was so charming, and initially I was drawn to him as a friend. At that time, I still didn't have too many friends in Turkey, so it was lovely having someone take an interest in me and offer to show me around.

After that, we were in touch almost constantly. He texted continuously, which I liked – it felt like he was really making the effort to get to know me. Gradually, we went on some dates and the relationship became romantic. It honestly seemed perfect at the beginning. He was so good at making plans, taking me for nice dinners and even buying me clothes. He would tell me I was so beautiful and made me feel amazing about myself. He reminded me of Boyfriend 2, who had always been so caring and thoughtful. What I didn't realise at the time was that Adam's behaviour was more like love-bombing. He was showering me with gifts even though he didn't have much money, and he was putting me on a pedestal. I've recently learned that narcissistic people build you up at first so that they can tear you down. (By the way, 'narcissism' is a term that can cover a multitude of personality traits. At the top end of the spectrum it's a psychological disorder, but when I use the terms narcissist/narcissism/narcissistic, I'm referring to them in normal speech as a way to describe the behaviour I encountered, and not as a medical diagnosis. Someone commonly described as 'narcissistic' tends to have a personality type defined by selfishness, a lack of empathy, and a need for admiration.) They want to control the other person and make the relationship revolve around them. One way they do this is through love-bombing, which is essentially the practice of lavishing someone with affection and attention, with the ultimate goal of manipulating them. At the time, though, I just thought Adam was a lovely guy. That's the problem with love-bombing – you usually can't work out that you've been love-bombed until it's too late.

The first time I noticed a red flag was a few months into our relationship, when we were staying in a hotel together for a weekend getaway. He asked to look through my phone. I thought to myself, *Why would he need to do that?*, but I didn't realise it was wrong for him to ask. And I knew I had nothing to hide, so I said, 'Sure.' Really, I should've said no. It's never OK for your partner to look through your phone. If you can't trust someone enough to respect their privacy, then you probably shouldn't be with them. I had never done anything to suggest I'd betrayed his trust.

He looked through my Instagram DMs, and noticed flirty messages I had received from random guys. Of course, I didn't respond to them. I said, 'I don't know them, they're just random people.' But he didn't like it. And then his behaviour started to switch on me. He became suspicious of every move I made, and started trying to control me, always questioning what I was up to and who my friends were. Now, I'm not saying it's controlling behaviour to check in on your partner and know what they're doing, but there was a tone to his questions that made me feel like he disapproved, and like I was always in the wrong. He would constantly accuse me of cheating, but I never did.

And the worst part was, he was accusing me of doing the very things that *he* was doing. He would promise to come home at a certain time, but then be out for all hours of the night. He'd follow random girls on Instagram. Later, I found out that he had been cheating on me the whole time – it turned out he had girlfriends in four different parts of Turkey. Basically, seasonal girlfriends for whenever he travelled. It's laughable to think about it now, but I thought he was suspicious of me because he genuinely loved me, and wanted to ensure I was as loyal as he was. I have since learned that this is a tactic narcissistic people use – they project their own wrongdoing onto you.

I didn't realise it at the time, but he was emotionally abusive in other ways too. He would criticise the clothes I wore. He didn't like it if I showed too much cleavage, and he would make me spin around before we left the house to make sure my thong wasn't showing. He told me I wasn't allowed to wear leggings. There was one time when he got really angry and he raised his hand to me. I said, 'I'm calling the police.' He stopped and he apologised, and we were back in love again.

I know it's easy to say, 'Why did you stay in this relationship? It's clearly unhealthy.' I would've said the same thing too. But if you've ever been in a relationship like this, you'll know how difficult it is to leave. You see, because of the love-bombing, we had formed a great connection. I was already in love with him by the time the red flags started waving. And even when he was mean or controlling, he'd also constantly tell me he loved me and reel me back in. He would justify his behaviour by saying he cared about me and was just being protective. I would try to tell him how hurt I felt by his behaviour, and he'd tell me I was exaggerating or being dramatic. I now know that this is a textbook case of 'gaslighting', which is when someone tries to make you question your own sanity or reasoning. I didn't know that's what it was called at the time, but I did know I was

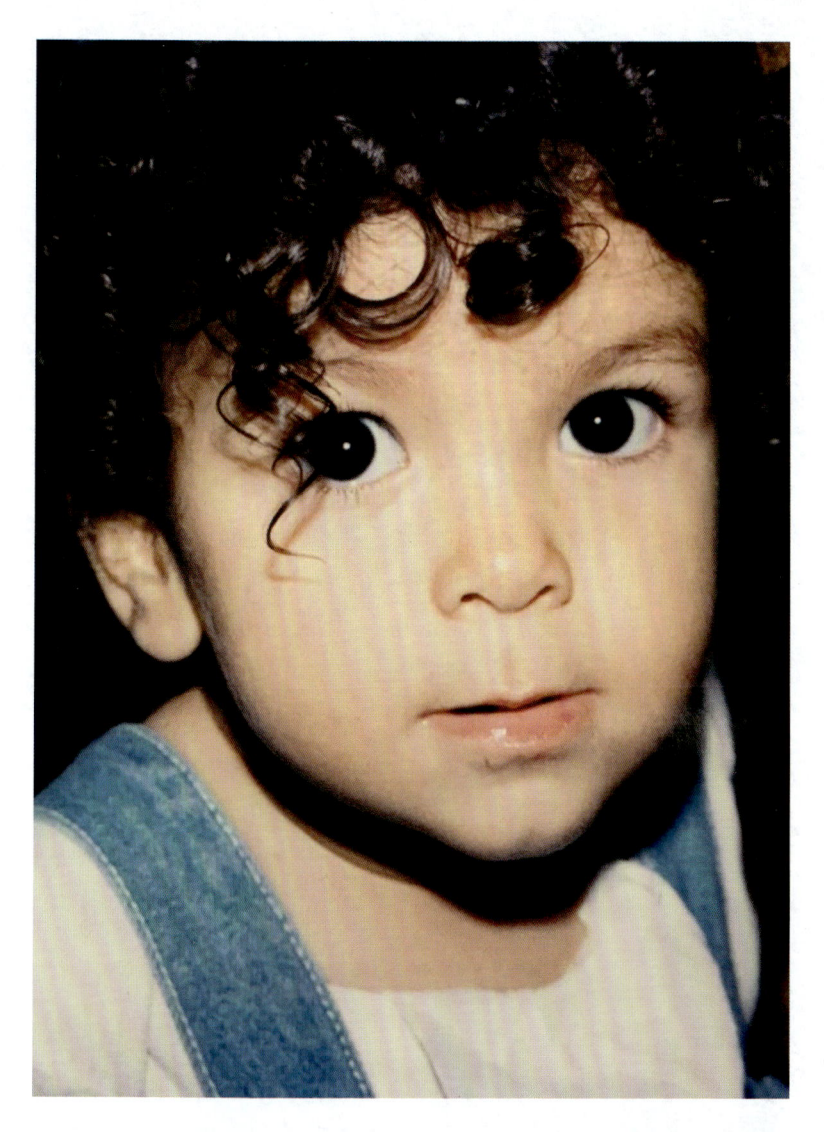

I love this picture of me, age three, with my big brown eyes and ringlets, patiently waiting for my lunch.

(above) Here I am as a baby with my mum and dad. I'm told I loved attention and being picked up all the time, and apparently everyone commented on those big brown eyes.

(left) Here I am as a two-year-old, enjoying a cuddle with my mum. My dad is behind the camera trying to make me laugh (and almost succeeding!).

Throughout my childhood, I always wanted to be more 'grown up'. I begged my mum to buy me fake nails so I could copy the dinner lady at school!

This photo was taken on the holiday to Ibiza I talk about on page 11. Talk about confidence! I'm so pleased my mum was able to capture this moment.

I've always loved Christmas – especially when I was a kid. Here I am on Christmas day, age six, at our house in Tottenham. I'm dressed up in the fairy costume I'd been given as a present. I loved it so much I'm pretty sure I slept in it!

This photo captures one of my cheekier moments. Despite the bird's nest on my head, I had refused to let my mum brush my hair. She had to chase me round the room with the hairbrush.

This was my first photoshoot, and I absolutely loved the whole experience. At just five years old I was really at home on set, and well behaved, but I also had so much fun – and I still feel the same today.

Like many young kids, I always wanted to play with my friends after school instead of doing my homework. Here I am after a day at primary school, in a standoff with my mum who was insisting I do my homework!

I did do my homework . . . sometimes.

I'm eleven years old here – at the start of those awkward 'tween' years. I remember this outing so clearly as my grandparents were visiting from Turkey and we were out for the day by the River Thames.

I've always loved being on stage and this was the first concert where I performed in front of a big crowd. I was fourteen and was so nervous, but also really excited to have my parents watching me from the audience.

My official school photo from year two at Risley Avenue Primary School. I loved those braids and used to get them done by one of the teachers at my after-school club.

walking on eggshells around him. I felt like I couldn't speak – I completely lost my voice.

I would tell my friends and family little snippets about his behaviour, and they'd all tell me I needed to get out, especially my mum. She was a therapist by this point, and she knew all about the signs of narcissistic behaviour. But I loved him, and I didn't know where to point the blame. I thought maybe *I* was the problem. When I'd tell him that my family were concerned, he would tell me that my mum and dad didn't really know what was best for me. He was attempting to make me distance myself from my family, which is another sign of emotionally abusive behaviour. Once you're isolated from all the people who love you, the narcissist can fully control you.

Eventually it came to a head when I was living away from Istanbul, working on that soap. He was staying in my flat at the time. It was my big break and I was so excited to be there, but it was tainted because he hated me being away. He knew he couldn't control me if I was out of sight, and he'd constantly raise suspicions that I was sleeping with a co-star or one of my producers.

Then, one day, he called me in a fit of rage while I was rehearsing. By that stage, my heart sank every time he called. Stupidly, I picked up the phone. He had found a bracelet in my flat that he said was 'proof' I'd been cheating on him. He thought it was a gift from another man, when actually one of my friends had bought it for me years ago. I was so confused and desperately tried to calm him down, telling him I hadn't done anything wrong. But he was too far gone – he was punching the walls, destroying my flat. He sent me pictures and videos of his hand covered in blood, saying, 'Look what you've done to me.' I was on the phone to him, shaking and crying, when one of the producers came over to me saying I was needed on set. I told them I'd come back soon, before hanging up on Adam and calling my mum and dad. 'I'm scared,' I finally admitted to them. They knew my relationship wasn't healthy, but until now I had been downplaying how bad it was because I didn't want to admit it, even to myself. By that point, though, I knew I couldn't go on any longer. I was genuinely afraid he might kill me.

My parents called the police and sent them to my flat to check on what was happening, while I tried to dust myself off and get back to work. I was living my dream, and I hated that he was trying to take that all away from me. When the police knocked, he answered the door and told them everything was fine before sending them on their way. But my parents helped me to get a restraining order, so he was forced to leave my flat. When the coast was clear to go back, I went with a friend, because I was so scared about seeing the state my flat was in. As soon as I walked in, I saw that everything was completely destroyed. I just burst into tears. I can't explain the feelings of anxiety, insecurity and helplessness that washed over me. I kept thinking: *This damage could've been done to me.*

I flew home to be with my mum for a bit after that. She gave me as much psychological help as she could, and I was put on anti-anxiety medication. One of the worst parts of the aftermath was that I felt guilty and ashamed that I had allowed the relationship to get that far. Every so often, the doubts would creep in: 'Was it actually my fault? Maybe *I* was in the wrong?' But it wasn't my fault – I was being manipulated. It could happen to anyone. I was just extremely unlucky, and I know that now. Support from my family and friends helped me through. I also noticed how much I had changed from who I was before the relationship. I had gone from being bubbly, lively and full of energy, to meek and afraid. I didn't wear the clothes I had once loved, and I had become less opinionated. I had lost my voice – and I knew I wanted it back.

The problem was, he normalised all those problematic things in our relationships. He normalised looking at my phone, and isolating me from my family and friends. He made me believe that all this stuff was just part of a loving relationship. But let me tell you this: if a man cares for you, he should want to elevate your life and support you. He should want you to spend time with your friends, achieve your goals and feel confident. Having been bullied as a child, my self-worth was so low that I was willing to settle for unacceptable behaviour. I believed these actions were signs of love.

Going In for Round Two

My friends, family, psychological help and medical professionals all helped me to move on from Adam. I went back to work, and threw myself into my career. I thought I was fully healed. But my mum warned me: 'If you're not careful, your next boyfriend could end up being a narcissist too.' She really helped me understand narcissistic traits, and encouraged me to read books about narcissism so that I wouldn't go back to the same place. I laughed when my mum said I could make the same mistake again – I thought I was aware enough now to spot the signs.

I hate to say that she was right. The problem is, once you've had a toxic relationship, it can become a comfortable place for you. You become used to the love-bombing and then the manipulation, because you've been convinced that that's what 'love' looks like. Even if, in your rational mind, you know that's not the case, you've almost become hypnotised. When you're in a relationship with someone who has narcissistic tendencies, it can also make you absorb some of these behaviours yourself.

And so in my next relationship – let's call the guy 'Ash' – I ended up in a similar cycle.

I met Ash when I was staying with my mum in a different part of Turkey, where I was getting my teeth done. I was bored one night, and there was a wedding happening downstairs in the hotel. My mum was getting fed up with my moaning about being bored, so she told me to go downstairs and join the wedding. 'Why not? Go and have fun,' she insisted. I thought, *Who the fuck joins a random person's wedding on their own?*, but at the same time, it sounded like just the kind of spontaneous fun I needed.

So I got down to the wedding, and made up a story about who I was related to, and just chatted with the various guests, laughing and drinking. It was such a fun experience, and they were all so welcoming. There was a really attractive guy who was making eye contact from across the room, but I wasn't interested in speaking to men – I was enjoying being on my own. Then the bride's mother, funnily enough, decided to introduce us. I started talking to Ash, and I was blown away by his charm. He was almost like a poet in the way he was describing himself and his life. His charisma and romanticism were intoxicating. At one point, my shoe fell off, and he picked it up and put it on my foot like I was Cinderella. It was like a romantic film, and I'm not going to lie – that drew me in. I thought: *Maybe that awful experience with Adam was just leading me to this . . . the actual fantasy I have always dreamed of.* In my childhood, I had always been one of the 'ugly sisters', so my Cinderella moment was validation beyond belief.

It was a similar story, but I didn't notice the similarities at the time. He asked me out for dinner, and seemed like the perfect gentleman. He suggested a few places to go for dinner, which I loved, as he seemed to want to take my feelings into account. He picked me up and said, 'You're the most beautiful girl I've ever seen.' At the meal, we got along so well – we were laughing so much, and he didn't stop complimenting me. I felt like I was being lifted on to the moon. Our first kiss, when he dropped me off, was so passionate and powerful. I honestly couldn't believe how romantic it was, and he had me hook, line and sinker.

He didn't live in Istanbul – we were staying an hour-long flight apart – but after the date, he said he wanted to continue seeing me. So we began a long-distance relationship, with him texting and calling me constantly, and me flying the hour to see him whenever I had the opportunity. He rarely came to see me; I was always having to fit in around his life. My mum warned me. She said: 'I can see the signs.' Initially, I brushed her off, saying he was nothing like my ex.

But then the warning signs became more obvious to me. I wanted to go on another Turkish soap, but he would say that I shouldn't pursue acting, that it was a dirty industry. He would say he didn't want me to be used. Like Adam, he made out that he was just being protective. Then he'd make comments about how much food I'd put on my plate. He would criticise the way I looked, even though I was going to the gym four times a week at that point. He'd pinch my leg and tell me I had cellulite (having cellulite is normal, by the way), and say I didn't look like the kind of person who worked out.

I've since learned that narcissists go after your weakest spot in an effort to break you down. I knew I had a great physique at that time, but he just wanted me to feel insecure. He knew about how I had struggled with my weight as a kid, and that I had a lot of trauma surrounding that insecurity. When he did this, I would put my foot down. I'd say: 'You can't speak to me like that.' But then he would act really caring to try and lure me back under his spell, and I'd forget how much he had hurt me. This would continue on and off for months, until I realised that I wasn't seeing friends any more, I was anxious 24/7, and I felt like my soul had been squashed again.

My mum had been warning me for ages, but I was too embarrassed to tell her I'd got it wrong again. I couldn't believe I had fallen back into a toxic relationship without even noticing. This was a man who went from calling me beautiful to telling me I was fat. I don't know how it happened. It suddenly dawned on me: *Wow, I'm in the same relationship, but with a different person. How the hell am I back here again?* I'd thought I was cured, that I had healed.

To this day, I still sometimes feel stupid for coming out of one toxic relationship and falling right back into another. I always talk about learning from your mistakes, and I really thought I was. But I think it's important for everybody to know that manipulative behaviour can still reel you in, no matter how strong you think you are. And when you've been in these kinds of relationships, and you're familiar with those hot-and-cold feelings and emotional abuse, it somehow feels safe to you. Recognising that – and knowing it's not your fault – is so important to help you heal.

My friends and my mum helped me wean myself off Ash as if I was a drug addict. To be honest, it felt like I was addicted to him. With their help, I completely cut contact and blocked him, which was much easier than it had been with Adam, as he lived in a different city, so I didn't have to worry about seeing him. I would always recommend that if you're coming out of a toxic relationship – you have to completely cut contact. Yes, you might get withdrawal symptoms and want to call them again or give them the opportunity for 'closure'. A lot of the time, toxic partners will try and make you feel guilty by making awful threats. But these are, mostly, tactics to manipulate you and draw you back in. You have to resist it, hold your head up high, and know that you can break free from them. They'll probably tell you that you're breaking their heart – but how can someone love you enough to be heartbroken by you, and at the same time treat you so badly? You don't do that stuff to someone you love. So, my advice would be this: no matter how much they guilt-trip you, stand firm and remember that your number-one priority is yourself, and your own happiness.

My Biggest Lessons

Anyone can fall into unhealthy relationships. In fact, I think most people have had at least one relationship that was extremely toxic, or where their partner was displaying narcissistic tendencies. And it isn't just men – women can be narcissists and can emotionally and even physically abuse their male (or female) partners. I'm only speaking about men here because that's my experience, but it can absolutely happen to anyone, regardless of gender or sexuality.

It can be really hard to spot red flags early enough, but I have some suggestions of what to look out for. Of course, I am not a professional or an expert, so this is simply based on my own experiences (and those of my friends). There's nothing wrong with a love-interest giving you attention and making you feel special – in fact, that's lovely when you start dating. But there's a line where it becomes over the top, like lavishing you with gifts early on, and making extravagant gestures. Narcissistic people are great at mimicking the ideas of romance that women want – those things we've all seen in the movies. But the reality is those grand gestures aren't what real romance is. Remember, you're living in reality, not a fairy tale. If it feels too good to be true, then it probably is. It's understandable to want to feel that electrifying, butterflies-in-your-tummy chemistry when you first start dating someone. But if someone doesn't give you that feeling, it could actually lead to a healthier relationship, because the best relationships build gradually from friendship and can then turn into deeper attraction. You can easily mistake lust and obsession for love.

The further you get into a relationship, the easier it is for someone to manipulate you, because by that point you have feelings for them, so they know you're more likely to forgive them for any bad behaviour. I know it's hard, but you have to keep your wits about you throughout the entirety of a relationship. It comes back to being your own best friend, and looking out for your own needs no matter what. Watch out for controlling behaviour or rude comments becoming normalised. That stuff is never OK – it doesn't matter how long you've been together.

And if you do think you're in an abusive relationship – whether that's emotionally or physically – reach out to someone you trust. I know it can be hard, especially if you blame yourself or think you're the problem. But your friends and family will love and listen to you, and they can help you to leave. If you're in a really bad situation, charities like Women's Aid and Refuge can also help. I'm so grateful that I had my mum and all her expertise, as well as friends who supported me through leaving. I was also lucky I had a job I could throw myself into as a distraction. Just because you're leaving what you know is an unhealthy relationship, doesn't necessarily make the heartbreak any easier. Look after yourself and protect your energy.

Both of my toxic relationships with narcissistic exes will leave scars on me for ever. I won't lie, those relationships changed me, and my walls went up. People sometimes tell me that I come across as guarded or cold, and they have a point because I have built a protective cave around me, for fear of falling for the same behaviours again. I changed so much about myself to make these men happy – men who, ultimately, I would cut completely out of my life. I am bitter about the time I wasted in those relationships, and I now find it hard to trust that people's intentions are genuine. Now, I notice actions more than I listen to words. But these experiences also made me more determined to fully heal and never get myself into situations like that again.

Sometimes, you have to go through the hard stuff to truly understand what it feels like. I know what it's like to feel misunderstood and like you're drowning, unsure about which way is up. I know how it feels to be shaking and terrified, to feel alone, rejected and unloved. But I'm grateful I have gone through those moments, because now I can recognise right from wrong. I've learned something from every single relationship I've been in, even the worst ones. I speak up more, I'm more independent and I'm better at setting boundaries. I wouldn't say I'm 100 per cent healed, but I'm on my way.

I think this mentality is why I was so clear-headed when I went into *Love Island*. I knew that having no relationship at all would be better than being in an unhealthy relationship. I wanted to meet someone who could complement my life, not control it. And ultimately, I never gave up on love. I had experienced a good relationship once, so I knew it was possible, and I never gave up hope of finding it again. Deep down, I'm still that romantic girl living in fantasy land and watching her favourite romcoms (albeit with some trust issues). You can still want love, and believe in love, while also knowing you're strong enough on your own.

Chapter 6

ALWAYS STAY TRUE TO THE REAL YOU

After lockdown, my life in Turkey was going pretty well and I was excited about the future. I had been offered a role in a movie, I was enjoying being single, and I was looking after myself. That said, I still really wanted to find love. I still had faith that I could find the right person; someone who was nothing like my toxic exes and made me feel good about myself. I was fed up with meeting people through apps and Instagram. I wanted to connect to someone on a deep level without any of that judgemental stuff getting in the way.

At around this time, I was chatting with my friend from the UK, who I had met years before while I was at uni. He's a celebrity manager, and we met at a public appearance for the *TOWIE* star Mark Wright in Preston. We got along, and we stayed in touch even while I was out in Turkey. He'd say: 'Ekin, you should come back to the UK. There would be loads of opportunities for you here.' But everything was going so well for me in Turkey that I always batted him away. Then, one day, when I told him about how much I wanted to find someone, he said: 'You should apply to *Love Island*.'

I laughed down the phone. I had watched bits of *Love Island* here and there. I knew it was a really popular reality TV show where singles lived in a Mallorcan villa with the goal of meeting someone, with the winning couple taking home a £50,000 prize fund. I knew there had been some amazing success stories from previous seasons, with some couples even going on to get married and have babies. And I did like the idea that *Love Island* is an intense way to meet someone – you can't get your mates to do the girl-code background checks, you just have to get to know them and be really present. But I didn't think it was the right place for me. First off, I was twenty-seven by that point, and I knew that the contestants were often as young as twenty, so I batted off the idea as a bit of a joke.

But then, a couple of weeks later, I had the most vivid dream. I was in the *Love Island* final, standing on a stage with the host, another couple, and a man by my side (although I couldn't make out any of their faces). The host announced the winner of *Love Island* and said: 'It's Ekin-Su!' There were fireworks, and I remember feeling so thrilled. I woke up the next morning feeling ecstatic, as if I'd really just won the show and found love, so I called my friend straight away to tell him about my dream. He thought it was hilarious – he didn't stop laughing for about twenty minutes. 'Ekin,' he said, 'I reckon you could get on to *Love Island* – but you'd be lucky if you lasted two weeks.' Still, he agreed that my dream was a sign, and said that I should apply to be on the show, just to see what happened. I thought, *What have I got to lose?*

Anyone who applies to *Love Island* goes through an online application first. There are endless questions about who you are, what you like doing on a night out, how your friends would describe you, how you deal with drama, what you want in a partner ... loads of things like that. I decided from the outset that I wasn't going to pretend to be some charming person – I was just going to answer every question completely as myself. I spoke about my bad experiences in dating, and my misadventures in acting and friendship, and I wrote about the type of person I wanted to meet: someone cultured, family-orientated, respectful and loyal. I know a lot of people say they just want to meet someone 'tall, dark and handsome' when they go on to the show. But I had been with people who were 'tall, dark and handsome' – and they were hollow on the inside, let me tell you. Of course, I know physical attraction is important. You want to have that initial spark with someone. But I had also been through enough in my life to know that a person's insides are more important than their outsides.

My manager friend helped me submit my application, and then a few weeks later, he heard from the *Love Island* producers. 'We really enjoyed Ekin's form,' they said. 'Can we do a Zoom call?'

I didn't know whether this step was a big deal or not, and assumed they probably had calls with thousands of potential contestants. But I joined the call and ended up chatting away with the producers for an hour. It didn't feel like an interview, it was more like a really fun conversation about dating and what I'm about. Still, I didn't think anything of it.

Months went by, and I completely forgot about *Love Island*. Rehearsals were starting for my new Turkish movie, and they wanted me to be one of the main cast members. My life was already on a solid track, so I honestly wasn't thinking about going on reality TV at all. I was mentally preparing myself to stay in Istanbul for a long time, and I was eating healthily and going to the gym to prepare for my role. But then, right at the start of summer, I got a call from the producers asking me to fly to London asap to meet the top bosses. 'What about your acting?' my mum asked when I called her to tell her I was getting on the next flight to London. It would be a big decision to leave everything behind. Still, I didn't know for sure that I had booked *Love Island*, so I thought I'd just go and see what happened, and then take the decision from there.

When I got back to London, I saw my brother before my big meeting. He encouraged me to have a shot of tequila for Dutch courage. I still have a video on my phone of me in my pyjamas, trying to get ready for my audition, with my little brother handing me the shot and winding me up. I guess I wasn't taking it too seriously because I didn't have a lot riding on it. My life was good already.

To be honest, my meeting was a bit of a car crash. It might have been the tequila's fault. I was even more loose-lipped than normal, and I'm pretty sure I said, 'Sorry, guys, I just farted,' as soon as I walked in the room. I was being almost too real, and I answered all their questions brutally honestly. As soon as I left the room, I felt so embarrassed by how it had gone. *But, oh well*, I thought. *It was a fun experience anyway.* So I flew back to Turkey the next day, and got back into preparing for my film role.

I was in the hairdresser's having blond highlights put in when I got the call.

'Ekin, you're in!' one of the producers said. 'You're going in as one of the first bombshells. You need to fly to Mallorca in two weeks. Pack your bags.'

I was completely in shock – they must've liked my realness after all. And I was also shocked by how quickly I squealed and said, 'Yes, I can't wait!' I had thought before that maybe I wouldn't do it if I was chosen, but in that moment, it felt like the right move for me. I thought maybe this was my time to meet someone genuinely nice, and have a fun, hot summer. My parents weren't sure at first, but eventually they agreed and supported my decision. *If it all goes terribly*, I thought, *I can just come back to Turkey*. People there didn't really watch *Love Island*, so I could just pick up where I'd left off. All I had in my head was that I just wanted to last two weeks.

'Just don't be the first one to get dumped,' my friend said.

'I'll try not to be!' I replied.

My Summer of Love

For the next couple of weeks, I went into overdrive getting ready to enter the *Love Island* villa. The first thing I did was go shopping (naturally). I knew I needed tons of bikinis, and sexy outfits for the evenings. That was basically the *Love Island* uniform.

When I arrived in Mallorca, I was introduced to my chaperone, a lovely woman called Emily. I was told that the producers match you with someone you'll get on well with, and we bonded straight away. This was a good thing, because I was told I'd be quarantining with just her for at least ten days. As well as ensuring you don't catch Covid (this was in 2022, when there were still a lot of worries about the pandemic), they also take your phone away from you and make sure you're not seeing news about the other people who are going on the show. It's also done to help prepare you for life inside the villa, where you're completely cut off from the outside world.

Emily and I stayed in a cute little villa with a pool and a garden, and I actually loved my time in quarantine. It felt like such a detox. We'd spend our days cooking meals together, chatting about life, working out in the garden and tanning.

Doing this little quarantine for *Love Island* showed me that I much prefer life without my smartphone (since then, I've done it for a few other TV shows where they confiscate your phone, and found the same thing). I really enjoy focusing on me and the people around me, and living in the moment. It's hard to do that these days, especially when my phone is so important for work, but it's so freeing when you can step away from it for a detox. People tend to think the idea of 'quarantine' sounds like torture (and often it is), but my time before *Love Island* was great.

I was never told exactly how long my quarantine would last – some people end up staying in quarantine for the whole season, only coming out right at the end to join the show. But I'd been told I would be an early bombshell, so I hoped it wouldn't be too long. On the first night *Love Island* aired, Emily was allowed to play the first episode for us to watch together. I remember watching the introductions and noticing the Italian guy, Davide. Obviously he was very attractive, but I thought: *Not for me.* I didn't like his intro; he came across like he really loved himself. He said he was loyal, but I laughed and said, 'Nah, he's not.' I really judged him at first, and thought to myself, *I'm gonna mess with this guy when I get to the villa.*

Then, the very next day, I was told it was my time to enter the villa – and I only had one day's warning! I thought, *Right, I need to look flawless,* so I asked Emily to help me decide on my entry dress. I knew people would judge me based on that first impression, so I wanted to look sexy but classy. In the end, I settled on a tight burgundy dress, which I thought was perfect.

The next morning, I woke up filled with excitement and anticipation. The producers came to meet me and I said goodbye to Emily – I was really sad to leave her, but so excited to get inside that villa. They took me to a secret location that was just outside the villa for me to prepare for my entrance. They had hair and make-up artists on hand, and told me what was going to happen. When I arrived, I learned I would walk in with another bombshell – Affia – which I was really glad about, as it felt less intense than arriving alone. They also said we'd both be going on dates with someone called Liam as soon as we got in. I remembered that he was quite young, so probably wouldn't be right for me, but still, I thought it would be fun to go on my first *Love Island* date and get to know someone.

As I was getting ready, I could hear screaming from inside the villa, as the Islanders were doing a challenge.

It was all starting to feel so real! But strangely, I didn't have any anxiety at all. I didn't feel any self-doubt, or any of the insecurities I've had in my head since I was a kid. I kept thinking to myself: *I've been chosen as a bombshell for a reason. I am more than good enough to be here.* When I met Affia for the first time a few hours before we walked in, she was much more nervous, so I tried my best to reassure her. 'Just pretend you're in a computer game,' I said. 'And have fun – don't worry about opinions from people on the outside.'

Walking into the villa, it did feel exactly like a computer game. It was so surreal! The villa was amazing, with all the brightly coloured beanbags and decor, just like I had seen on screen. It was such a rush going on the date and meeting everyone for the first time. And, I kid you not, I forgot the cameras were there after about thirty minutes. I just thought, *This is going to be such a fun summer.*

It's quite a strange experience arriving as a bombshell, because – even though it had only been a couple of days – everyone had already bonded and (supposedly) formed connections, so I was an outsider right from the get-go. I noticed girls whispering about me and getting defensive about the boys they were coupled up with, and I knew some of the guys didn't really know how to take my level of confidence. I remember saying to Davide: 'Hey, Mr Muscle, I'll see you in the gym at 6am, yeah?' and he later told me he thought I was so annoying! But thankfully, I was used to being an outsider. Nothing anyone said or did could convince me I didn't belong, so I just got on with it.

From the moment I entered the villa, I felt drawn to Davide. Even though it was funny to wind him up, I liked the fact we were both from the Mediterranean, and I got the sense that there was a deeper, more vulnerable side to him that I wanted to draw out. We were both judging each other massively: he thought I was spoiled and overly confident; I thought he was self-centred and only wanted to show off his abs. But still, there was a magnetic connection that made me think I wanted to get to know him better.

You'll probably know that Davide ended up becoming a huge part of my *Love Island* experience, and I honestly wouldn't change any of it. That said, there were definitely some ups and downs. But even some of the downs ended up becoming pretty memorable moments, as I would find out on the other side. The first one was when another bombshell, Jay, came into the villa. Davide and I had flirted a bit by that time, but he was still coupled up with another girl, Gemma, and I couldn't really tell if he was interested in pursuing me. I decided there was no harm in exploring other options. Although the new guy Jay wasn't necessarily my type, I thought I'd give it a whirl.

I wanted to pull Jay away for a chat without the judgemental eyes of the villa watching us, so I thought: *What's the most private place in the villa?* It was, of course, the terrace. But you could still be seen if you were standing up, so I insisted that we crawl along the terrace to hide ourselves. I later found out that my crawl was pretty iconic.

I wasn't trying to be a sneaky villain, and my aim wasn't to kiss Jay behind Davide's back. I just thought it was common sense to try and hide from the other

Islanders, because in real life you wouldn't normally have so many eyes on you when you're just getting to know another person. But it didn't go down particularly well with the other Islanders when it all came out, least of all Davide, who – unbeknown to me – had started developing feelings for me. That's when another iconic moment happened. He shouted, 'You're a liar! You're an actress!' Although it was hurtful at the time, I saw the funny side not too long after. It has also been hilarious seeing other people's reactions to this scene since, and how quickly it became a viral meme.

It took a while for Davide to trust me after that, but eventually he warmed up. I loved how we could be really silly together and would often chase each other around the villa, playing pranks. Even when we weren't having deep conversations, I felt like we could communicate without speaking. There was undeniably something there. I won him over just before the dreaded Casa Amore, where the boys and girls were separated and tempted with new Islanders. I knew I had already messed about enough, so didn't feel the need to pursue any new boys, but I was really disappointed when I got back to the main villa to find Davide had kissed two girls. It was yet another test, but we made it back even stronger.

Meeting Davide was the most incredible part of being on *Love Island*, but I'd be lying if I said it was the only highlight. The whole experience was just unforgettable. Being in the villa felt like being on a different planet – you're not allowed to know what the time is, which can be disorientating, but it was also a really welcome escape from reality. You just woke up when they put the lights on. Sometimes it could be super early if we had to get up for a challenge, and you'd only know how early it was because the sun would just be rising outside. It was nice not knowing the time; it made the days fly by.

The only other way to tell the time was by when meals appeared, though they never really showed mealtimes on the show. We were very well looked after in all aspects. We spoke to mental health professionals almost every day to check in with how we were feeling. We'd also have one day off per week, where there wouldn't be any challenges or recouplings, although we were still filmed for the *Unseen Bits* episode that aired on Sundays. Girls and boys were separated, and it was an opportunity to have our clothes washed. We could also order McDonald's that day, which was a real highlight!

Every day, apart from those days off, there would be some sort of drama. We were always waiting for that distinctive 'ding' of a text message to tell us about a challenge, or a new person coming in, or a recoupling. As the series went on, I did bond with some of the other girls, and I liked to take on the motherly role in looking out for them. I always told the girls to know their worth and not let people walk all over them or judge them for just being themselves.

I think the reason I am where I am today is that I kept it very real the whole way through. I remember there was one occasion when I noticed that all the other girls' partners made them coffee in the morning, but Davide would never do that for me. I went into the Beach Hut and was really upset about it – I didn't even think it would be aired, because I knew it seemed like such a non-issue. But I also knew that it wasn't about the coffee; it was what the coffee represented. I felt like he didn't care for me in the same way as the other partners, and that's what made me so upset. I later found out this caused a lot of discussion in the outside world. There were people who really related to me and how I felt in that moment, because they'd had similar experiences. Sometimes the smallest thing can make you cry. And there were people who berated me for being a spoiled brat. In the end, you won't be liked by everyone, but at least you're staying true to yourself. I made mistakes, but no one is perfect. And I think it's good for viewers to see people fucking up, then apologising, then rebuilding connections – just basically being human. No one can maintain being perfect the whole time. It's so unrealistic.

That said, I believed there were more people who hated me than loved me throughout the series. There was one time when I was in the bottom two, after the whole Jay saga. I was up against Amber. When it was between us two, I truly believed I was going home. I was pooping my pants at the firepit that day. But even when Amber went home and the public saved me, I still didn't have an inkling of how much support I was getting in the outside world. Inside the villa, the other couples didn't seem to believe in me and Davide. We'd always be voted the 'least compatible couple' and things like that. Because we argued and we weren't always rock solid, people didn't believe we really had something. But actually, I think that's even more real, because conflict is normal in relationships.

Regardless, I didn't let the other Islanders' opinions affect me. I knew I was falling for this man, and he was falling for me, and I was just so grateful and happy to be having that experience. And if we got booted out of the villa, so be it. When we went on our final date near the end of the series, there was a singer and candles everywhere. It was the most romantic thing I had ever experienced in my life – it was just like a movie. How could I worry about all these outside opinions when I was able to have this life-changing experience? I felt like the luckiest girl in the world.

When the Dream Becomes Reality

When I made it to the *Love Island* final, I had actually completely forgotten about the dream I'd had when I was still in Turkey. I was just living in the moment, not thinking about what had come before and what might come next. I wasn't thinking about winning, because having Davide by my side, and with all these incredible memories, I felt like I'd already won. But the whole day was so exciting. We got to pick our outfits, and I chose a glamorous, sparkly dress that made me feel amazing. It was our first show with a live audience, so it was surreal hearing people's cheers for the first time after we'd spent so many weeks separated from everything.

In typical Ekin-Su style, though, my experience just before I went on stage wasn't as glamorous as it seemed. A few minutes before I was due on stage, I was desperate for a pee and begged the producers to let me go. The only problem was, my dress had to be sewn on to me, as there was no time to tailor it, so I couldn't lift it up to pee. One of the show's runners came into the loo with me to try and help me, and there was no loo roll either. In the end, I had to just open my legs and wee on the floor, so I was basically wetting myself, and there was pee dripping down my legs. I was desperately trying to wash the wee off one minute before going on stage. So yes, Davide and I were announced as *Love Island* winners while I stank of pee!

When Laura Whitmore built up the tension before announcing our names, my heart was beating so fast and I had the biggest smile on my face. Davide believed we were going to win, but I didn't think we would. When we were announced as the winners, it felt like I had won the lottery. I couldn't believe it! The excitement was incredible. It felt wild that so many people had liked me enough to vote for me to win. So you can imagine my surprise when I later discovered we had received the highest percentage of votes in *Love Island* history, taking sixty-three per cent of the vote in the final four couples. It was the biggest high point of my life, and is still one of my most treasured memories. I had gone through my life believing I wasn't enough. Not pretty enough, not normal enough, not British enough, not Turkish enough . . . but all of those feelings slipped away. The public had essentially told me I was enough – and it was an amazing feeling.

After the announcement, we drank and partied before an even more exciting part of the night – Davide and I got to stay in a hotel room for the first time without cameras watching us. I won't go into the details, but I think everyone knows what happened ... and it was great. And the next day, we were finally given our phones back. I freaked out for a second because I couldn't remember my passcode. It had been so long! Straight away, Davide and I exchanged numbers. It was crazy that we had built up such a connection over our weeks together, yet still didn't even have each other's numbers. Then the team said, 'Ekin, check your followers!' I already had a big following on Instagram thanks to my acting in Turkey – around 300,000 – but I couldn't believe it when I saw my follower count was 2 million. It almost felt like a weird glitch. But then I saw all the incredible messages of support from my followers, and I started to believe it was real.

That day, while we were still in Mallorca, all the finalists had a day with the press and welfare teams, offering us advice about how to navigate our new-found fame. We were coached on the kinds of things that had come out about us in the press already, and advised on how to cope with the trolls. They warned us that, although it would all seem exciting, there would be lows as well as highs. I'm so grateful to ITV for taking me under their wing.

I took in everything they said, but I was also riding high on the win, on having a boyfriend, and also having £25,000 dropped into my account! It was the most money I'd ever had in one go, and it felt absolutely incredible. I was so excited to get home, and the journey back to England was even more wild. There were fans stopping us at the airport to ask for pictures, which was unlike anything I had experienced before. I had been recognised occasionally in Turkey, but this was something else. There was so much buzz and hype around me and Davide. I can't explain the feeling of arriving in Stansted Airport to banners and crowds. Our families were there to greet us, too, and seeing my mum and dad so proud was really special.

But I didn't have too much time to sit back and enjoy all the positivity. It was go, go, go from the minute I landed. There were a lot of brands that wanted me to be their new face, which was so cool, but it meant I was constantly in meetings, signing contracts and making public appearances. The first night Davide and I stayed together in London to go on *Love Island*'s spin-off show, *Aftersun*, we were papped for the first time. We were both like lost puppies – it was all so overwhelming. Davide was like my safety net in those first few weeks, and I would get separation anxiety when I wasn't with him. It felt easier to navigate this crazy change in our lives when we were together.

It was during this time that we properly fell in love. It was nice being able to get to know each other away from *Love Island*, to see what our lives were really like. We met each other's families and realised how similar our backgrounds were. I think the moment I knew I was in love was when we were both in New York City about a month after *Love Island*, looking up at separate billboards we were on – mine was for the clothing brand Oh Polly, his was for Boohoo – and we just felt so proud and grateful to be together to experience this. It brought us even closer.

But the downsides of fame we had been warned about were also becoming clearer. I lost a lot of friends during those first few months. People who had known me for a decade had sold stories about me to the press. It was very sad and disturbing to see, but it taught me a lesson about what true friendship is. Real friends wouldn't sell you out for the sake of a few thousand pounds. If they really needed the money, they could've asked me for help, instead of throwing me under the bus. Thankfully, I had already grown a thick skin following my experiences at school, but it still hurt – and it reinforced the walls I had built around myself. It reminded me that I can't trust people, and I'll always have to be my own best friend.

I also realised how fickle people could be, and how some people would want to use my new-found fame for their own benefit. So-called 'friends' I hadn't spoken to for years would suddenly reappear and ask me for a coffee, while other reality stars tried to befriend me for the sake of increasing their own follower counts. It can be such a fake world, which makes it really hard to know what people's intentions are. I even started questioning the intentions of people I was working with – agents, managers, PR teams – who were supposed to be on my side. They'd always give me advice and tell me which moves would be best for my career, but then I'd think: *Is this actually something I want?* Sometimes, it felt like everyone wanted a piece of me, like I was an object that could be bought and sold. Everyone is your friend when they want something from you. That's something I've learned gradually throughout my journey since *Love Island*, and we'll come back to it later.

It took time to adjust to being a recognisable person. Obviously, there was so much good that came from it – I felt like I had a whole community of people who loved and supported me, and had my back. But then there were the trolls.

I'd always thought I was immune to name-calling thanks to all the bullying I'd experienced in my past. But there was a time when I got a bit addicted to searching for myself online, and then reading the comments sections. People's cruel remarks would get stuck in my head. I knew I was sending myself into a spiral of negative thoughts, and I needed to protect my sanity.

Coming Back to Earth

The biggest challenges of fame came a bit later, and I'll go into that more in the next chapter. But one realisation I came to very quickly is that it's hard to be authentic in this industry. You might think that being a reality star or influencer is so glitzy and glamorous – and don't get me wrong, some days it is. But you also become dehumanised. I was no longer just 'Ekin-Su, the Turkish girl from Essex', I was 'Ekin-Su: the brand'. It can be very lonely, especially when you don't know who you can rely on. I was lucky I had Davide during this time, but I can imagine for a lot of people, it's really overwhelming.

I know a lot of people in this world say that fame hasn't changed them, but I don't think that's ever possible. I can definitely say fame changed me. I am not the same girl I was before *Love Island*. Some people might say I'm a diva, but I would say I'm more sure of myself – and I'm not ashamed of that. I think having the validation of winning reminded me that I should know my worth, and set boundaries when I need to. There were a lot of things I said 'yes' to in the aftermath of *Love Island* that I probably shouldn't have (again, more on that in the next chapter). I should've really had some stern conversations with myself about what I wanted, and what I needed. But I've learned my lesson. Now, when someone offers me a work opportunity, I'm much more discerning about their intentions, and take time to think about whether it's the right thing for me. I ask myself, what do they want from me? Do they have the best intentions? Are they bullshitting me?

We could all benefit from having these conversations with ourselves. It's so easy to get swept up in the excitement of new opportunities that we forget to stop and check in with how we're actually feeling about everything. Just because something is a great idea on paper doesn't mean it will work for you. It's all about listening to your gut instinct and trusting that you know best when it comes to your own life. That's something I have kept on learning throughout my adventures in fame, and to be honest, it's something I'm still working on now. I try to put my foot down if things don't feel right, but it's challenging.

Since becoming a 'celebrity', I've realised just how image-focused our world is, especially on social media. Of course, I knew this before, but it's even stronger now. There's so much pressure to be on social media, and to always look like you're living such a cool and interesting life. I feel pressured to put content out, even though social media isn't really my forte. I'm not an influencer like other reality stars; I'm not as good at the stylised, perfectly curated photos. That's just not me. And anyway, I've already said that people who do post like that aren't necessarily showing what's real. Life isn't always glamorous and gorgeous, even for celebrities. And I think it has a bad impact on the people who see this content, because they end up thinking they have to prove that they have a nice life too, instead of just living in the moment. I massively appreciate my fans, but I don't live my life just to please them – that would drive me crazy. And you shouldn't live your life to prove anything to anyone else, either.

I'd love to tell the younger me that celebs aren't the happiest people, and they don't have everything, even if it looks that way. Of course, so many of the things we get to experience are incredible blessings. But there are downsides, too, like losing privacy and control over your life. And I think success will only make you happy if you love what you're doing. Just because you're earning money, it doesn't automatically mean your life will be better. Take it from me, as I've experienced both sides of the coin. In those early months, I spent a lot of money on clothes and bags, and eventually, I realised that they were just boosts of happiness that didn't last. It was a short-term hit of dopamine. Now I know it's more meaningful to spend my money on experiences, pushing myself out of my comfort zone, and looking after my mental health. I am grateful for everything that I have, and I would never take it for granted, or forget that I am blessed.

I know being in the spotlight like I am isn't the norm, but I think the lessons I have learned from fame can apply to everyone. Don't be too trusting of people who want something from you, but always trust yourself. Prioritise your own happiness and sanity, even if it's not the thing other people think you 'should' do. Staying true to who you really are will get you far. It might seem scary, but other people respect and relate to people who are honest and real, especially because we live in such a fake world. Appreciate the things about yourself that make you different. Accept that you can't please everyone, but as long as you're staying true to you, you'll always be OK.

Chapter 7

IT'S OK TO STRUGGLE – EVEN WHEN YOU HAVE 'EVERYTHING'

Before I went on *Love Island*, I had struggled with my mental health at a few different points in my life. There was the bullying when I was at school, the early heartbreaks, and the toxic relationships that made me feel anxious and low. Throughout all the hard times, I had invested in myself and protected my energy by leaning on my mum for advice, reading self-development books and working out. During low times, I'd go on YouTube and watch videos about how to feel more positive and how to stop overthinking. Even if they didn't offer any valuable tips, it just made me feel better knowing that other people were searching for the same things as me, and going through what I was going through. Reading forums would remind me that there was nothing wrong with me, and that everyone goes through these emotions. When times were tough in my own life, I'd throw myself into supporting other people, which always made me feel good. I always managed to find my own way out of difficulties to find the brighter side. I was confident and felt comfortable in my own skin.

It might seem strange to say that one of the hardest

times in my life came a few months after I won *Love Island*. My life had just changed massively – and mostly for the better. I had experiences that the younger me could only have dreamed of, and I had more money in my account than I could've wished for. The support I received from strangers was incredible. I felt it in the streets when people came up to me to say 'Hello,' and also online when I looked at my phone and saw their comments and likes. I felt validated by so many people who loved and believed in me. But, as I already touched on in the last chapter, sometimes getting everything you've ever wanted isn't all it's cracked up to be.

I want to be very clear that I'm so grateful for everything I have, and I know I was so blessed when I came out of the *Love Island* villa. The show was not the cause of my internal struggles. To be honest, I think part of the reason it took me so long to admit I needed help was because I was embarrassed. I didn't want to seem ungrateful, especially when I knew others were struggling a lot more than me. Maybe you have experienced this too. Maybe you've been through a time in your life when everything was going right – you had the loving relationship, or the great job, or the fun social life, or all of the above – but you felt lower than ever before. You might have felt ashamed to admit that you were not OK. Maybe you felt like you couldn't tell anyone you were unhappy because you didn't have a real 'reason'. But I'm here to tell you that those feelings are valid. It happens to the best of people, and it's important to be honest about it.

So, here I go.

* * *

I've already mentioned that life was a whirlwind when I came out of the villa. I was shocked by how quickly everything happened, how quickly I seemed to go from being a normal girl to something else altogether. One of the first awakenings came as I was trying to navigate my new relationship while in the public eye. If you've started a new relationship, you'll know it can be very delicate in those early days. You're working each other out, and learning where to set boundaries. You have to figure out where the lines are drawn between friends and family giving you advice because they care about you, and other people sticking their noses into something that they don't fully understand and is none of their business. Having a public relationship came with all the same problems – except it was like those problems were put under a magnifying glass. Instead of a few external opinions, Davide and I had thousands of people watching our every move and making comments about us. The press teams on *Love Island* had warned us about this, and ITV had looked after us so well, but nothing could have prepared me for the level of scrutiny.

The first time it felt really bad was when I was out in LA with my assistant Georgia, doing a photoshoot for one of the brands I was working with. I was on such a high, busily working away, and feeling so excited about being in Hollywood (as a born performer, you can imagine this had been a dream of mine since I was a little girl!). But when I got into bed one night, I noticed I had received a DM from one of my fans. They wrote, 'You might want to watch this,' followed by a link to a TikTok video. I had received lots of random things in my DMs that I had mostly ignored, so I'm not sure why I felt compelled to click the link. I think something in my gut was telling me to look.

I opened the video and saw it already had hundreds of thousands of views. It showed Davide with two girls, and the headline said something like: 'Davide seen with two blonde girls going out after a boxing match.' It wasn't that, in itself, that had me worried. I clicked on the comments and saw what lots of people were saying: 'He's clearly cheating on Ekin-Su.'

Confused and shocked, I dropped my phone on the floor and ran to Georgia's hotel room, which was just down the hallway. When she opened the door, I burst into tears. I know it could've been nothing, but my gut was telling me something wasn't right. And I hated the idea that all these people who didn't even know me were speculating about whether my boyfriend was cheating on me. It was humiliating. It felt like everything flooded back from my childhood: the insecurities, the loneliness, the doubts . . . all those emotions I'd felt all those years ago. I know it sounds irrational, but I had this overwhelming feeling that people were laughing at me and saying, 'You're not good enough. Not for Davide, and not for anyone.'

Georgia tried her best to calm me down. 'Look, you're working in LA right now, and it's an amazing opportunity,' she told me. 'Let's deal with it when you get back. It could be something innocent – don't assume the worst just yet.'

But I couldn't stop myself – I rang Davide straight away, but there was no answer. Eventually I sent him a message saying, 'How could you do this to me?', but I didn't get much out of him, he simply replied something like 'Excuse me?'. The next day I had no choice but to push on with work. I had to do the photoshoot with a mask plastered on my face, pretending everything was fine. That was the start of my 'work face'; I trained myself to leave my worries and problems at home and not let anyone see that I was suffering. I don't think this is unique to being in the public eye. Lots of us do this. Showing that we're upset can seem like showing weakness, which isn't the 'professional' way. So, we just go to work and get on with it, and we push our real emotions deep below the surface.

Later, I spoke to Davide again and he told his side of the story. He said it was innocent and nothing had happened (I still had a feeling something was off, but we'll come back to that later). I chose to trust him and brush off the rumours, but this incident was a big moment of realisation for me. I knew now that we couldn't do anything without people watching us and scrutinising us. We were ripe for criticism and speculation, and people would dig to find whatever they could if it sounded like a good story. For the rest of that trip in LA, when I should've felt relaxed and excited, I was so anxious. I was constantly careful, knowing that people could be taking pictures of me at any moment. I was cautious even to interact with male waiters, because I was worried that something I said could be captured and misinterpreted. I knew I would never do anything disloyal in a relationship, but the thought of rumours spreading weighed down on me.

Not long after this, there was another big turning point: I was asked to appear on *Dancing on Ice*, the celebrity ice-skating competition show. Weirdly, I had seen rumours swirling online that I was going to be a contestant before I'd even heard anything about it, and my fans didn't seem too happy about it. I'm not sure why there was so much negativity, but I think there was a general feeling that it was too soon after *Love Island*. I think my fans sometimes know what's best for me!

When the offer came in, I hesitated. I didn't want to let my fans down. I also knew how busy I was, and this would be yet another thing to add to my plate. But I asked my team's advice, and everyone thought I should go for it. I reasoned that I might not be offered this kind of opportunity again. Also, I knew I wanted to eventually do some presenting work, or even go back into acting in the UK, and this show would introduce me to a whole new audience. Plus, I actually loved ice skating. I grew up going to skate at Alexandra Palace in London with my parents every winter. My mum reminded me how much I loved gliding around on the ice, and I thought, *Maybe everything happens for a reason. Maybe this is my destiny!* I knew it would be hard, but then I hadn't thought I'd win *Love Island* and I'd somehow managed that. So I decided: *Fuck it. I can do anything I set my mind to.* So I ignored the niggling feeling that it would be too much to take on, and I said 'yes'. When it was announced, a lot of my fans were disappointed. But I knew you can't impress all the people all the time, so I just put out a message saying I hoped they would understand and support me, and I started preparation for the show.

Of course, I had been told that it would be a big commitment. But I don't think I understood just how *much* of a commitment it would be until I got started. I had no choice but to throw myself into it and remind myself I could overcome challenges, but I was completely exhausted. I really wanted to do well on the show, but I also wanted to do well in my other projects, and didn't want to let anyone down. At this time, Davide and I had also moved in together in London, which was another thing I had to deal with: buying furniture and organising everything. He was busy too, but his schedule was much more flexible, and I was jealous of how much time he could spend chilling. I came home so late every day during the pre-show training that there was only time to eat my dinner and go to bed.

I know it might seem strange, but *Dancing on Ice* was much more of a mental adjustment than *Love Island*. While I was in the villa, I was cut off from the outside world. My character and relationship were being criticised, but I couldn't actually see it at the time. I could just focus on getting to know Davide and having fun, without all the outside noise. *Dancing on Ice* was different, because I had access to the internet and the newspapers throughout, and people could still speak to me in the street. I was constantly made aware of other people's opinions. It really weighed on me. And as much as I'd loved ice skating before, the level of pressure sucked the joy out of it. I think my body was numb when I was dancing. I was leaving it all to muscle memory, and I couldn't really connect with what I was doing.

It didn't help that I received a heap of criticism my very first week on the show. The first song I was assigned was 'Toxic' by Britney Spears. Obviously, it was an iconic pop song, so I was excited to do it. There was also a move in my choreography that involved me crawling across the ice. Given I had become known for my *Love Island* crawl, I thought that was a funny addition. But viewers complained that my dance and outfit (which showed quite a lot of skin) was inappropriate, I was put in the bottom two that week. It was so disappointing, and really got me down. I hated that I was being judged on my costume, the song choice, that crawling dance move – and probably the fact I had been on *Love Island*. I felt like I was being slut-shamed, to be honest. Women should never be shamed for what they wear and how they move.

When I made it through to the next week, I insisted that the producers give me some wholesome songs – so I went from sexy dancing to 'Toxic' to dressing like a nun for *The Sound of Music*! And funnily enough, I got through without being put in the skate-off. It was a whole new world and a new audience. I realised not everyone is so accepting. In the end, I got halfway through the series before being eliminated. I'm really proud of myself for making it that far.

But while I was on *Dancing on Ice*, and in the months that came after, my mental health was rapidly spiralling. I was burnt out. It's such a shame that I wasn't able to properly appreciate being on that show. The younger Ekin-Su, who had skated for hours around the rink, would have been so excited by the opportunity, and all the amazing people I got to work with, and be trained by. But I was just doing so much, and I was too tired and felt too much pressure to take it all in. I had barely any time to work on my new relationship. I had no time to decompress with family and friends. I wouldn't say I regret it, because there were some incredible high points, and I'm proud of how far I came in my skating. That said, if I was given the chance all over again, I probably wouldn't do it. I'd trust my gut in knowing how much work is too much to handle. It was just too soon after my last reality show. I've learned that you can't do everything. I used to think saying 'yes' to everything was a sign of strength, a sign of a 'go-getter' attitude. I still believe that, within reason. It's good to push yourself out of your comfort zone. But there's also power in saying 'no' and understanding your limits. Back yourself and trust that you're making the right call. You know yourself better than anyone, and don't ever forget that.

During this time period, I felt like I didn't have many friends I could lean on. As I mentioned in the last chapter, the world of fame can be a fake and lonely place, and I really learned that the hard way. I had already lost friends who had sold stories about me, and I didn't know who to trust. My guard was up, but at the same time, I craved friendship. It hit me one day when I came home from a job and was feeling really sad. I picked up my phone and scrolled through my contacts, looking for someone to call. I knew I had my family and Davide, but I just really needed a friend. I realised there was not one person I felt I could call and open up to. That's when it hit me that I was so lonely. It took me back to my school days, when I would eat my lunch alone in the toilet cubicle. I was so different to that girl – I was a grown-ass woman and (dare I say it) famous – but the feelings were virtually identical.

They say that it's lonely at the top, and I didn't understand that before – but I do now. So many people knew who I was, and I was at the top of my game, and yet I didn't know who to turn to. On the streets, I would look at groups of friends and feel jealous of people who had these trusting, carefree bonds. It was suddenly so hard to make new friends, because I was no longer just a girl introducing herself; I was Ekin-Su, the girl from *Love Island*. People didn't look at me in the same way.

I knew I was incredibly lucky to have so much love, support and validation from people who had watched and followed my journey, but while I appreciated that massively, it was never quite the same as having real-life friends. Even when people are asking you for pictures, you can still feel lonely. It's not the same as making deep, meaningful connections. People only know a fraction of your life. They don't know you enough to be a friend.

I still find it hard to make friends today. I'm always second-guessing what people want from me. I've been let down so many times over the years, by people I thought I could trust. Now, I put people on trial. I'll make up a secret and tell someone, and then see how fast it gets around. If it doesn't come back around, I'll know I can trust them. I know that sounds super paranoid, but I'm just trying to make sure I don't get burnt.

I remember one particular occasion, I was with Davide in an airport. While he was queuing for the gate, I went to the loo and just burst into tears. I can't even remember why, but I know I just felt so sad. As I came out of the toilets, I heard someone shouting, 'Ekin, Ekin!' There was a fan who had recognised me, and was coming over to speak to me. My eyes were still wet from crying, so I quickly grabbed my sunglasses from my bag and put them on. As they came over and said, 'Oh my god, I love you so much,' I had to swallow a lot of saliva so I didn't sound like I'd been crying. I chatted to the fan a bit and thanked them for their support, and then the tears came rolling down again as soon as they walked away. I didn't feel like I could show emotion in front of any of my fans, because they all knew me as the sassy, confident Ekin-Su I had been on TV.

I had never felt so lost as I did at this time. Everyone seemed to know who I was, but I had no idea. I had so many people pulling me in all directions – I felt like I was a toy being fought over. Everyone seemed to want me to be a certain way. I felt like I was a product, a money-making machine. I just said 'yes' to everything and had no boundaries at all. I would touch my skin and know I was there, but at the same time, I wasn't aware of my own senses. I knew I existed, but my soul wasn't connected to me.

Seeking Help

After a few weeks, my mum and those closest to me noticed that I was spiralling downwards and wasn't myself. The first thing they noticed was that the spark was gone from my eyes. I had always been such a sparkly, excitable person, but that had just ... gone. The next thing they noticed was how low my energy was. I barely went out and often wanted to be on my own. It was a far cry from how I used to be, always the life and soul of the party. I was overthinking a lot and was incredibly paranoid. I'd ask the same question so many times to make sure I felt confident enough going into a job. I could switch on the charm when I needed to, but the people closest to me knew I was hiding how I was really feeling. I have always struggled with my mental health, and my inner child was being triggered by this new life, and it was bringing a lot to the surface. Things that I hadn't dealt with before *Love Island* were being unlocked, and I was overwhelmed by change, expectations and not trusting anybody's true intentions.

As I've said before, I didn't want to seem like I was ungrateful for the amazing life I had. I was forcing myself to keep going, and kept reminding myself that there are so many people in worse situations than me. I had to keep telling myself: 'You wanted this life, and now you have it.' I felt guilty for how I was feeling, so I tried to push it away. In a way, it was similar to when I was bullied at school, and I was too embarrassed to tell my parents that I wasn't doing well. I have always wanted to seem like I have everything together. But the people who love and know you more than anyone can tell when you're hiding something.

They knew I wasn't happy. A key symptom of depression is when you no longer find enjoyment in the things you used to love doing, and that happened with me. I could be in the most beautiful places, doing the most incredible things, and they felt average. I beat myself up about it, but the truth is I wasn't in the right mental state to enjoy my life. I wasn't being ungrateful or silly. It wasn't my fault.

I'd had psychological help in the past, partly because my mum is an amazing psychotherapist. But she knew that she couldn't help me herself; and I needed to speak to someone objective, and someone who specialised in the realities of fame. I started seeing an amazing therapist who helped me massively. It made such a difference being able to open up and be honest with someone about how I was feeling. For too long, I had let all my emotions bubble up inside, and that's never a good idea. You might think you have a handle on them, but actually it all adds up and can mean you sink lower and lower. You have to address the things you're struggling with, so they don't get worse.

Therapists won't necessarily solve all your problems, but they help you understand more about yourself, which can lead to really helpful realisations. She helped me work through a lot of my childhood trauma, and I came to understand that the abandonment issues I have from not being accepted as a kid can mean I now struggle to set boundaries, and can be a bit of a people-pleaser. She reminded me of the strong, confident and unique person I am. She told me that you can be a strong woman and still be vulnerable. We can't all be strong 100 per cent of the time. One exercise that made me cry was when she told me to give the young Ekin-Su a hug. 'Tell the younger Ekin that you'll keep her safe; tell her you're all grown up now, and you're loved,' she instructed me. I learned that sometimes when I feel sad, it's because of the little girl I once was, who needs love, validation and connection – because we all need those things. Reassuring the 'little me' helped the grown-up me, too.

In the end, I was in therapy for about a year and a half, and can honestly say it was life-changing.

You should never feel ashamed to seek professional help, whether that means going to therapy or speaking to your GP about taking medication. There's still a lot of shame around mental health – so many people think admitting that you're in therapy or on medication is a sign of weakness. But I think it's really brave and powerful to be able to say, 'I'm not OK, but I'm working on feeling better.' I wish people did it more, because we all struggle. We all have times when we feel low, whether that's because something really bad has happened, or for no reason at all. You don't have to justify your sadness or anxiety. You can just admit it's there, and work on ways to deal with it.

If you're unable to access therapy at all, my first piece of advice would be to reach out to someone you love. I know it can be hard to make that step. Even though I am super close to my family, I still found it challenging to admit I wasn't doing well. If you feel lonely, tell someone. I can guarantee the people who love you will respond and want to make you feel happier whenever they have a moment. People are dealing with their own lives, and won't always notice if you're sad, but the moment you open up, you allow others to help you. Don't just assume that someone doesn't care because they haven't noticed. Make the first move and reach out.

Social media can be a negative place if you feel low, that's for sure. All that comparing your own life with other people's can make you feel bad. There's nothing worse than lying in your bed feeling like shit, and scrolling through endless videos of people on glamorous holidays having the time of their lives, or bragging about some exciting career achievement. I have been there many times. But you can also use social media for good. You can join communities of people who talk about positivity, happiness and self-development. The more you click on these kinds of uplifting posts, the more you'll see that stuff on your feed. At the same time, you might choose to mute or say 'not interested' to any accounts that make you feel worse. Setting boundaries applies to the time you spend online as well as in the physical world. Say 'yes' to the good things that make you feel happier, and 'no' to the bad things that make you feel crap.

Alongside seeking help from other people, there are lots of things you can do to pull yourself out of a dark hole. In other words: you can be your own best friend. When life feels like it's spiralling out of control, I focus on what I *can* control. And that means putting more time and energy into healthy habits, including exercise and sleep.

Prioritising Healthy Habits

I have already mentioned that I took up running when I was a teenager. I loved how it helped me get out of my head and into my body. I enjoyed the adrenaline rush and the fact that it made me feel productive, even if I did nothing else all day. But I will admit that a big reason I laced up my trainers was because I didn't want to go back to being the 'fat kid'. Running is known for being the best form of cardiovascular exercise – which helps you work up a sweat and lose weight – so I stuck at it because I thought that was my only option for staying slim. When I was young, there was so much pressure to look a certain way. I thought that was the whole point of exercise: to look good. Otherwise, why bother?

At the time, I thought I looked amazing. But looking back at pictures of myself, I think I looked ill. I was doing some pretty unhealthy crash diets, so I just wasn't getting the right balance of vitamins, minerals, protein and carbohydrates to support how active I was. I looked like I was wasting away.

When I met Boyfriend 2 at university (the good example of an ex!), he introduced me to strength training. I had always believed that women shouldn't do weights, as they make you look bulky and masculine. Given how set I was on being small, that didn't seem like a good idea. But he told me that you need to gain muscle if you want to burn fat – and, not only that, it makes your whole body healthier. I still wasn't sure, but we went to the gym together and he showed me how to use some of the machines, like the leg press and pull-down machine. He also showed me how to do some basic exercises like biceps curls, and squats and lunges while holding weights. I had to use the lightest weights for everything, but I couldn't believe how good it felt. I swear, after only one session I looked in the mirror and was adamant I could see muscle definition that wasn't there before.

The next day, my whole body burnt, but I was hooked. It wasn't just about how I looked, I loved how it made me feel. He then introduced me to doing different exercises on different days – dividing them into leg day, arm day, abs day, and back and shoulders day – and I felt like such a boss when I was able to gradually increase the size of the weights I could handle. It gave me such a sense of achievement knowing that I was getting physically stronger every time I went.

When the pressures of fame and relationships became overwhelming, I leaned on exercise to help me through.

Fitness – and especially strength training – is a great form of discipline. You have to be really consistent with it, otherwise you won't notice any improvement. Sticking to a routine gave me back faith in my own abilities. It reminded me that I can do anything I set my mind to. When I finally managed to lift a weight that previously seemed *so* out of reach, I experienced a dopamine high like nothing else. I thought, *I did it! It was my hard work that got me to this place!* Feeling like that, even when the rest of my life seemed chaotic, was a very powerful thing. It offers a reminder that you're doing fine, and that anything is possible.

To get good at any kind of exercise, you have to find your groove and make it a commitment that becomes part of your daily life. It's not just something you do in January, or because you're going on holiday, and then give up. When you push through the pain of the first few sessions and you find good times to exercise or go to the gym – whether that's first thing in the morning in your living room, or popping into the gym on your way home from work – it becomes really easy to make it part of your day. And the great thing about routine is it gives your life structure. When life gets tough and everything feels out of control, routine can be a godsend.

For me, it's a really mindful experience. When you work out while listening to music or a podcast, it's the best opportunity to escape the world. With strength training in particular, you really have to focus on how your muscle feels in every movement, so it takes your mind off all of the problems you have, and instead focuses it on what your body is doing. It's a great way to stop overthinking, because you're connecting your mind with your body.

I have found that I feel emotionally stronger when I'm physically stronger. That's why I recommend strength training to everyone I meet. It makes me feel confident and unstoppable. If you can squat a heavy weight, you know that you can also stop texting that guy who is messing you about. If you can hold a plank for a few minutes, you know you can also hold on to your morals and boundaries. You realise just how much strength is already inside you. It reminds you that you can do hard things – and you'll keep this mentality with you in your work, relationships and general life. It helps you to believe in yourself.

Maybe start by trying a few strength exercises at home – you don't have to use dumbbells, try using items like water bottles and tins. Once you feel ready, you could book a class or a one-off session with a personal trainer to push yourself and learn more. It's all about feeling empowered with knowledge because the less you know about fitness, the scarier it will feel.

That being said, I know that fitness is difficult to start, and to stick with. But the mental and physical health benefits are worth it. I recommend pushing yourself out of your comfort zone. Try something new. Just because you tried running or cycling in the past and you hated it, doesn't mean you won't find something else that you like. I don't believe anyone can hate all forms of exercise – you probably just haven't found something you enjoy yet! There are so many ways you can ease yourself into new forms of fitness with apps and YouTube videos. Plus, classes and personal trainers can be so motivating. These days, there are tons of amazing studio classes you can go to, many that combine strength and cardio, and have cool lights and amazing playlists. If you find it difficult to stay motivated when you work out on your own, going to a class might be the thing for you, because you end up feeding off all the energy from the instructor and the other people in the room.

Don't be disheartened if you don't enjoy the first thing you try. Everyone has different things they will like, and your favourite form of fitness won't be the same as other people's. I know I have raved about strength training, but it might not be for you – and that's OK. You can still find your own way to move your body that makes you feel empowered, energised and strong. Any form of movement can count as exercise. Maybe, for you, that's going to dance classes. Dancing releases so many endorphins and makes you feel so happy! Perhaps it's using a skipping rope – the kind you used to use in the playground as a kid. Jumping rope is a good form of cardio as it gets your heart pumping. Or maybe it's going for regular walks, and getting out in nature. There's the added benefit of being in green space that makes you feel positive.

I like working out by myself because it feels like a good escape from the pressures of life. But it's really nice to work out with friends too. Whether it's going to a class together or just helping each other at the gym, it can make you feel more motivated if you do it with someone else. I love helping my friends with their workouts, which makes me feel good about myself too. Also, you can combine it with getting a smoothie or a coffee afterwards. Giving yourself a treat at the end of something hard will always make it feel more enjoyable!

If you do choose to work out by yourself, my biggest piece of advice is try to forget about everyone else in the room (if you go to a gym) and focus on what you're doing. The reality is, people aren't judging you as much as you think they are. They're focused on themselves and what they're doing, and so should you be. Yes, there will be the odd time an annoying person will comment on your form or tell you something you already know, but just ignore them and get back to focusing on yourself. I think a lot of people get put off by the gym because they imagine they're going to be watched and scrutinised. That's really not the case. You can be in your own bubble. No one actually cares about how fast you're going on the treadmill or how heavy your dumbbell is. And even if they do, remember that your health is more important than what other people think.

I would also advise creating a great playlist for your workouts. You can find ready-made ones on Spotify, but I think it helps to choose songs that you know make you happy and boost your mood. I love seventies and eighties music, so my playlist is full of Cher, Led Zeppelin and the Rolling Stones! Yours will be completely personal to you. I know lots of people really enjoy listening to podcasts. There are loads out there at the moment, from funny interviews to true-crime dramas. They can be great at distracting you when you're doing a sprint on the treadmill or doing your twentieth squat that might otherwise feel impossible.

Your workout routine will probably look different to mine because your life and schedule are different, and so are your preferences. Maybe you prefer to go on a morning walk every day, and then do two classes a week at your local yoga studio during your lunchtime. Come up with a plan and routine that works around your life, and makes you feel motivated and excited. Workouts shouldn't feel like punishments or a chore – they should always make you feel better, not worse. Don't beat yourself up if you miss a session – just dust yourself off and keep going. It's like playing an instrument – you will get better with practice, and it'll become easier. Whatever you choose to do – just move as much as you can. It's so important for your mind and your body.

Sleep is also really important to me. It's such a basic thing that we all know we need, but we often forget the impact it can have on us. If I have worked all day and then only slept for four hours, I can guarantee I'll feel horrendous the next day, physically and mentally. Everyone needs a different amount of sleep, and I've worked out that my sweet spot is seven hours. This isn't always easy to achieve, though. The more responsibilities I take on, the harder sleep becomes. I overthink a lot, and if I've had a busy day, I'll replay it all in my head when I'm trying to drift off. And then, when you're worried about not sleeping enough, that can make sleep even harder.

The way I deal with it? I always spray lavender onto my pillow, and I'll even take it with me if I'm travelling. It's so soothing and helps me drift off. And I try to simplify my evenings, so that I feel calm and relaxed before I go to bed. I'll light my candles, drink honey and lemon tea, chat to my mum (who always makes me feel reassured), put on relaxing music, do my skincare routine and put my phone on sleep mode. When I can, I avoid scrolling on my phone before bedtime too. It can get me into a negative spiral if I see news stories or captions that make me feel sad or anxious. It's so much better to protect your energy and turn off all notifications before you go to bed. Instead, I like to wind down by watching videos of positive affirmations on YouTube and Netflix documentaries, or reading self-development books.

If worrying and overthinking is really keeping me up, I'll sometimes get out a notebook and pen, and write down all the things I'm grateful for. Appreciating everything you have really helps. Sometimes I think: *Why am I complaining?* I am in such a fortunate position. I tend to worry about things that haven't happened yet. I make up scenarios in my head. But there's no point worrying about something that might not even happen. Just remind yourself that if the worst does happen, you have all the strength you need to deal with it. There's no point mulling over tomorrow – just live it when it comes. I also use sleep meditations sometimes – there are lots of apps that offer hypnotic stories that send me straight to sleep.

Sleep is so important that I would always say to prioritise it over almost anything else if you feel you haven't had enough. So, if you need a nap in the day, have one. In my opinion, having a nap doesn't make you lazy – if your body wants to sleep, listen to it! It means you'll have more energy to tackle the rest of your day. Equally, if you think your body would benefit from skipping a gym class in order to get another hour of sleep, do it. Have that lie-in on the weekend if you need to catch up after a busy week. You know your body best. You should never feel ashamed of resting. We're taught that we always have to be go-go-go, but we won't function properly unless we recharge our batteries. You put your phone on charge every night, so think of sleep as putting yourself on charge, too.

Put On Your Oxygen Mask First

Talking to someone about how you're feeling – whether that's a professional or just someone you love – alongside exercise and sleep is important. But there are so many other things you can do that count as 'self-care', and they'll be unique to you. Maybe you love crafting and making collages. Or maybe you love reading novels. Self-care isn't just about doing the things other people do, it's about doing what makes you feel calm and well rested.

Self-care might mean being with your friends – spending time with people you love can make you feel re-energised and supported – but it's also important to get comfortable with things you can do on your own. It's more quiet and peaceful, and it also makes you independent. If you can have a night in by yourself and really enjoy it, that's an amazing way to be your own best friend. It's a reminder that you can make yourself happy, by focusing on the things you love. You don't have to worry about impressing or entertaining other people. You only have to worry about impressing and entertaining yourself – and that's freeing. If you don't enjoy your own company, how will you ever be happy? You'd make an effort with a new partner or friend when you want to build a relationship with them, so have the same attitude when it comes to the relationship you have with yourself. If you've had a stressful week, plan a gorgeous evening in, alone. Run a bath, buy your favourite food for dinner and watch your favourite movie.

People often think 'loving yourself' means being arrogant or having a big ego. I don't think it means that at all. It simply means you respect and value yourself enough that you don't need as much from other people. Of course, it's always nice to be validated and supported by others. But, in an ideal world, you wouldn't feel so reliant on that, when you have everything you need to be your own support system. You can love yourself, and make yourself happy, just as any family member, friend or partner would do. This is something I have to keep reminding myself, too.

Often, people don't stop and think about their mental and physical health until something goes wrong. You might not consider doing back stretches until you're struggling with pain from being hunched over your computer. You might not think to rest until you're completely burnt out. It's better to get ahead of it, and prioritise your health right now. Focus on prevention, rather than just cures. I lean on self-care even more during difficult times, but I try my best to fit it into my day whatever happens, because I know I'll feel the benefits in the long run.

You can't live your life to please everyone else, and you can't wait for happiness to just show up at your door. You have the power to create your own happiness, from the inside out.

We all face so much pressure to be perfect, emotionless robots. That applies to everyone, not just people in the public eye. There's a pressure to always appear confident and strong. We live in a world that can make you feel like you're weak if you open up and admit you're not always OK. But it doesn't mean you are weak – it just means you're human.

Thankfully, I think the world is changing. So many more people are opening up about mental health struggles. Personally I find it really comforting when people share their stories, even if they seem to have the most perfect lives on the outside. When you think about it, many of us have the same struggles, whether we're in the public eye or not. We feel exhausted from work. We feel overwhelmed by our schedules. We have to navigate relationships and friendships, and make time for our families too. We worry about the future. We have to deal with difficult people and bullies. We listen to the news, and we're bombarded with gossip and scary stories. No wonder our brains can't cope with it all. No wonder we shut down every once in a while. In my opinion, we all need to take the time to step back, reassess, remind ourselves of who we are, and come back to the world with a renewed sense of energy and excitement.

It's easy for me to say all of this, but of course it's not easy putting these lessons into practice. Difficult times would come again, as you'll discover in the next chapter, but at least I'd know that I had all the tools to make it through.

Chapter 8

EMBRACE THE ROLLER-COASTER RIDE

*A*ll my life, I have craved love – from family, friends, partners and strangers. But I haven't always known what healthy love looks like. Growing up as a lonely kid without a sense of belonging, I thought love meant having someone validate me and tell me that I'm good enough – or pretty enough – for them. This has sometimes meant I've been too trusting, and too reliant on other people to make me feel good about myself. When someone shows me the slightest hint of kindness, I ignore any red flags, because I'm scared that if I don't pick up those crumbs of love, then I won't have any at all.

On *Love Island* and throughout my career in the public eye, I have tried my best to project an image of myself as independent, strong and sassy. I want people to think, *Ekin-Su doesn't need anyone – she's got this all on her own.* That's not entirely true. In fact, I've probably been lying to myself. That's the Ekin-Su I *want* to be, but it's not necessarily the Ekin-Su I am right now. I'm a work in progress. I don't have it all figured out. None of us do, really! It took a particularly turbulent time in my life for me to realise that.

The End of the Fairy Tale

After winning *Love Island*, I truly believed I had completed life, and that all my dreams would click into place. I thought this was it: no more bullying, no more feeling unworthy, no more toxic relationships with terrible men. I thought I had found my knight in shining armour, and we'd gallop off into the sunset and live happily ever after. Sadly, real life isn't a fantasy romance book – as much as I wish it was.

I have already spoken about how Davide and I grew even closer after we came out of the villa. We'd had this big, crazy experience together, and it felt like he was the only person who understood the journey I was on. I really loved him – probably more than I loved myself. Looking back, I think I lost myself in the relationship. I was giving all my love, time and energy to my work and to him, and I didn't have any left to give to myself. I was running on empty, and I wasn't receiving the same love back that I had been pouring in.

There were a few things that happened throughout our relationship that made me lose my trust. These events would knock my self-esteem, which would make me even more reliant on validation from the jobs I was doing, and from my amazing followers online. But that insecure voice was always there, telling me: *Your boyfriend doesn't want you. No one wants you.* It made me feel paranoid and insecure. But I kept holding on – because when it was good, it was great. We had a strong connection and had shared so many lovely moments I didn't want to throw away. I was still that hopeful, happy girl who had won *Love Island* alongside her partner in crime. For a while, I thought our relationship was only getting better and stronger, and that nothing could break us. I desperately wanted it to work. But then, in 2023, I was hit with the biggest betrayal.

That summer, I went through quite a traumatic health issue. It's not something I'm ready to speak about right now, but maybe I will when the time is right. Afterwards, I felt terrible – both emotionally and physically – so I went to Bodrum in Turkey to escape with my family and two of my Turkish friends. I needed to get away, take some time to recover and be surrounded by people who could see past the Instagram filters, and who would know when I wasn't OK. Davide was working in Manchester and was heading to Ibiza during the same period, so he couldn't make it. Alongside dealing with this health problem, I felt anxious about him and what he was getting up to out there. Looking back, I was so vulnerable, and kept having these feelings that I wasn't 'good enough' to stop him straying. News stories and social media posts alleged that he was cheating on me, but I didn't want to believe it. Our relationship had become toxic, from both sides. The child inside me was crying out to be loved, to be pretty enough, to not be abandoned. But I was also angry, and I would react from a place of pain. All those core beliefs about myself that I had learned from a young age – *you are not enough, you are ugly, nobody likes you* – had resurfaced, and I was scared.

Towards the end of my trip, I was feeling a lot better, and my friends took me to a beach restaurant for some much-needed food, cocktails and sun. One of my friends brought her boyfriend along, so I was friendly to him, and we were all chatting away. I didn't think anything of it. But someone in the restaurant had filmed this innocent chat, and the video made its way to Davide. The next morning, he called me to drop a bombshell: he was breaking up with me. He was accusing me of cheating on him, which was categorically untrue. I still don't understand how he could accuse me of that when he knew very well what I was going through emotionally and physically at the time. As I tried to explain this to him, I was told that a statement would be going out on social media announcing the break-up. It felt so sudden and cold, especially after everything I had been going through, and the various cheating allegations that had plagued our relationship in the past. I dropped the phone and fell to the floor, crying hysterically.

I was not OK. I became a child who couldn't self-soothe – I didn't know what to do. My comfort blanket had been my boyfriend, and I felt like that had been ripped away from me. My mum came into my room to see me rocking and shaking hysterically, and she tried her best to comfort me. Within two minutes of the call, the statement had been published online, and only a few minutes after that, news sites had published headlines about our break-up. It was a massive shock. I didn't even have a moment to process what had happened before the whole world knew. To this day, I still can't make sense of why and how it happened. My mum thought he was looking for a reason to break up with me, and that innocent video became the excuse. But I don't think I'll ever really know.

I came back to England feeling low. I felt like there was a part of me missing. I came home from the trip that was supposed to heal me feeling ten times worse. I was crying every day. I was barely eating, and I didn't want to leave the house – not even to go to the gym, which had always been my safe space and the one thing that could make me feel better. My friends Grace, Simone and Mabel would come every day to check up on me. I know they were really worried about me, because I was saying things like, 'I don't want to be alive any more.' I know that sounds dramatic, but I had been consumed by this man, and the fairy tale he represented – a fairy tale that I was still clinging on to. He had become the centre of my life. And because of the industry we're both in, I was constantly being exposed to pictures of him, and people were always texting me with rumours and gossip about his party lifestyle. I would see pictures of him with other girls, and I would spiral and compare myself to these beautiful women. I would scroll endlessly to see what they looked like and what they were doing, and I felt threatened. I would think: *Why am I not good enough? What's wrong with me?* I wanted to be 'the one', but I felt like I was replaceable. Once again, I felt like that little girl who was never pretty or cool enough to be picked.

It fills me with shame to admit this, but it's important to be really honest. It's a process so many women go through when they break up with someone they love. We have a tendency to think it's all about us, wondering what we did wrong, and thinking of all the ways in which we weren't good enough. We then use other women as proof of our own insecurities. Obsessing about these other women is a horrible, vicious cycle that only makes us feel terrible about ourselves. If I could go back to that broken, numb girl lying in bed, crying and staring at her phone, I would take the phone away from her, and tell her not to go down that road. It only leads to heartache and never-ending comparison. I'm not sure she would've listened, though. When you're stuck in that self-hatred and shame loop, it's very difficult to escape it.

The only reason I got out of this funk was that he came back. Yes, a few weeks later, we reconnected at a party, and we got back together. I know what you're thinking: *Why would you go back there, when you had been so badly hurt?* It comes back to what I said before – I was so desperate for love that I was willing to accept crumbs. The break-up had been such a shock, and I wasn't ready for it. Just hearing him apologise to me, and say he loved me, was enough for me to forget about how insecure and sad I had felt. I was addicted to him, almost like a drug – one hit of affection, and I would happily throw everything else away. It made me feel safer being in that relationship.

Our relationship had started in the most intense way possible. We had spent weeks of solid one-on-one time together, and had then emerged into this 'celebrity' lifestyle. We had probably been through more in one year in our relationship than many couples go through in five years. It was all accelerated. We'd had the highest highs and did everything together. When you have invested so much in a person, you don't want it to go to waste. It can feel like a failure to let go of everything you've built. He represented the fairy tale, and I believed in it. Even though any rational person would say, 'This isn't a fairy tale,' my head was still in dreamland.

I still didn't fully trust him, and I was scared that he would abandon me again. But I pushed all my doubts beneath the surface and tried my best to keep our relationship together. Then, a few months later, I headed to a beautiful castle in Scotland to film the American edition of *The Traitors*. I was so excited about this opportunity, so I attempted to set my relationship issues to one side in order to really enjoy the experience. You probably know all about the concept of *The Traitors* since it has become such a phenomenon, but if you don't, the idea is that a big group of people live in a castle together. Most of the contestants are Faithfuls, but there are some Traitors living secretly among them. The Traitors must 'kill' the Faithfuls one by one, while the Faithfuls must try and identify the Traitors. If there's a Traitor left in the final, they win the prize money, but if the Faithfuls manage to get rid of all the Traitors, then they win.

It's basically like a real-life game of *Cluedo* – you have to act like a detective, and you're never sure who to trust. I loved the whole vibe of it, as I'd always dreamed of playing a role in an Agatha Christie drama. The castle was so eerie, and it felt like we were in a movie. The US version was made up of all celebrities, mostly from American shows, and I made so many friends. I met incredible people of all ages and backgrounds – I even struck up a bond with the former politician John Bercow! They all seemed to accept me for who I was, and I had such a great time being a Faithful and trying to suss out who was lying. Like with *Love Island*, I loved the fact I wasn't allowed my phone during filming. I always feel a bit more free when I'm disconnected.

Sadly, halfway through the series, I was 'killed' by one of the Traitors. But it was one of the most transformative experiences I've ever had. Most of the time, when Faithfuls were killed, it would be in the night, and they simply wouldn't show up for breakfast the next morning. My 'death' was a bit different. The previous night, I was handed a cup to drink from, which I didn't know was a poisoned chalice. And the next day, we were all told we had to wear black and go on a funeral procession. The challenge was to work out which person from the group had been poisoned.

Of course, it's only a show, but it was so well done that everything felt unbelievably real. The group had to decide which three people may have been poisoned, and those three people had to get inside coffins in the woods, which were ready to be lowered into the ground. I was chosen, and made my way over to one of the coffins. Honestly, it was so scary. For a moment, I was fully embodying this role. As I lay in the cold, uncomfortable box, it felt like my life was flashing before my eyes. It made me reflect on my own life. I thought: *This is what life is. You're here, and then you're gone.* I looked up and all I could see were trees. I listened to the sound of the birds while I waited for the announcement of who had, in fact, been 'killed' by the poisoned chalice. The show's host, Alan, announced my name as that person – and then the lid of the coffin abruptly closed. I was left in pitch darkness, apart from a small camera light that beamed at me from the corner of the coffin. I could hear people throwing dirt on top of my coffin, and it genuinely felt like I was being buried alive.

I stayed in there for about an hour while the rest of the cast finished filming the funeral above me. I couldn't hear anything, and in a weird way, I had never felt so calm and peaceful. It didn't matter how I looked, or whether I was good enough for my boyfriend, or what was going to happen once this show was over.

When the coffin was finally pulled up and they opened the lid, the light was blinding. It was like I had just gone up to heaven. That serene feeling was replaced by a rush of overwhelm, and I immediately burst into tears. I had never cried like that in my life. It was partly sadness for everything I had been through up until that moment, but also a kind of spiritual awakening. I had felt lost for so long, and I knew I needed to find my way back to myself, one way or another. Something had to change – I just didn't know what yet.

I couldn't stop crying for about three hours. Just like with the amazing *Love Island* production team at ITV, I was well looked after by the aftercare team. When I was finally ready to reconnect with reality, I was handed my phone. All I wanted was some love and support from my boyfriend. I had just been through the most incredible (and intense) experience, and I craved that familiarity and comfort. I wanted someone to ask me how I was, and tell me everything was going to be OK. But the first thing I saw when I was handed my phone was a headline about Davide, who had been spotted on a night out with a girl who had found fame on the adult-content site OnlyFans. Once again, I was hit with the familiar feelings of unworthiness, wondering why I could never measure up to these beautiful, sexy women. I looked in the mirror and I hated myself. You're meant to feel good about yourself in a relationship, but I felt the opposite. (OnlyFans, as a platform, would become a trigger point for me and something that would make me feel extremely defensive. But more on that later.)

It hit me like a train. I didn't want to deal with this constant anxiety any more. Of course, I didn't actually have a near-death experience on *The Traitors*. But in some ways, it felt like that – it felt like I had been given another chance at life. I thought: *Why am I settling for a relationship that makes me feel so unhappy?* I wanted to come home and be showered with affection, but instead I had to deal with these headlines, and him assuring me he'd done nothing wrong. I knew this wasn't what I wanted, but I still didn't know how to make that change. Even after all I had learned from past relationships, it still felt difficult to leave.

Instead, I became quieter with him while I sought advice from my loved ones and my therapist. Sometimes you need to get out of your own head and seek support from people who know you best. When December rolled around, I still hadn't made a decision. We had planned to visit Italy – where Davide is from – over Christmas, and I was bringing my mum and brother as well. I decided to go. I think a part of me hoped maybe this trip would rekindle things and bring us closer together. Instead, it did the opposite. While on a day out in Rome, he decided it would be funny to 'fake' propose to me. It was heart-breaking for me to watch this man get down on one knee in front of me, as if it was the real thing – but not because he actually wanted to marry me. He just thought it would be a laugh. I felt mocked in front of my family.

'It's just a joke, baby,' he said.

I said, 'Is this really what you think I'm worth? Who is this funny for?'

As someone who has always dreamed of the fairy-tale romance, it felt like a slap in the face. After a huge argument erupted outside the Coliseum, I ended up leaving Italy early with my family, devastated by how the trip had turned out.

A few days later, I was meant to be going skiing in the Italian mountains with Davide and a few friends for his birthday. I know that a normal person wouldn't go back, not after everything that had happened. But I felt guilty. It was his birthday, and I had planned some lovely things for him. So, I put pride to one side (and ignored my family, who begged me not to go), and I flew back to join the group for the ski trip. It wasn't all terrible. He could be really sweet to me on the slopes (I was a newbie skier, and kept falling over!). I knew that there were these lovely sides to him, and those are the sides I fell in love with. Now, though, I had a sense of clarity. These moments of sweetness weren't enough. I needed better love. I knew that this would be the last time I'd see him. I knew it would be heart-wrenching, but I needed to walk away.

It still took a bit of time before I finally worked up the courage to say, 'It's over.' During that time, we spoke on the phone and over text. I knew that I couldn't see him, because if I did, I would forget about everything I had decided. I was very vulnerable and weak around him, and I knew I needed to stay strong, otherwise we'd sink into our same patterns again. I had to make a list of everything he'd done, all the things that I had given him second, third and tenth chances on. I had to read it over and over again, to remind myself why it was the right decision. When we eventually published the statement confirming our break-up at the end of January 2023, I felt relieved.

'Ekin-Su, You Have Been Evicted'

After things ended with Davide, my life was such a whirlwind that I barely had time to stop and think about it. I was flying back and forth to the USA for press events surrounding *The Traitors* (which had aired in January), and my brand work kept me busy. And then my manager presented me with the opportunity of appearing on *Celebrity Big Brother*.

This social-experiment show – where a group of people live in a house together and are forced to 'nominate' each other for eviction, at which point the public vote for who to evict – was not something I had ever pictured myself doing. Of course, I knew how big it was when I was growing up, but I wasn't the kind of person who had watched it religiously. I knew that they were rebooting the show after it had been off air for a while, so there was a lot of hype around it. The main reason I said 'yes' is because I felt like I had something to prove.

Because my break-up had been such a long time in the making, I convinced myself that I had already processed it and healed from it. I told myself that I was independent, strong and capable without a partner, and *Celebrity Big Brother* felt like a good opportunity to prove that to the world – and to myself. I'd had my big break in reality TV on *Love Island*, but that was all tied up with Davide, and represented the whole wild journey we'd gone on together. I felt like I needed to do something else now I was single, just to prove to myself that I could.

If I'm being really honest with myself, I was also looking for a distraction. I wanted to throw myself into something to escape from all the rumours and pictures of Davide that were swirling online. I thought that separating myself from the drama was a show of strength, but deep down, I had never felt more weak. I was extremely damaged, hurt and vulnerable. My heart was broken, but I was in denial about the impact this was having on me. In hindsight, I shouldn't have taken part in *Celebrity Big Brother*. It was just too soon after my break-up.

But hindsight is a wonderful thing.

I was genuinely excited to enter the *Big Brother* house. I've mentioned before how much I love being surrounded by people of all different ages and backgrounds, and that I tend to connect with older people because I want to absorb their insights and life experiences. I gravitate towards people who have more life experience than me, in the same way I drifted towards my teachers' classrooms when no one my own age wanted to talk to me at school. The day I entered the house, I was fizzing with excitement about the journey ahead. I felt hopeful about the friends I'd make and the new experiences I'd have: experiences that would have nothing to do with my ex. It wasn't my goal to win or to play a game. I had been so busy in the lead-up to entering the house that I'd barely had time to think about it.

My main aim was that I wanted people to see the real me. The only problem was, I still didn't know who the 'real me' was. As much as I felt excited to take part, when I walked into the house, it suddenly felt like the first day of secondary school, when I had been so desperate to fit in. Ever since I was a kid, I've always felt like an outsider and feared that no one will understand or 'get' who I am. I don't think those feelings ever leave us. I wanted to be liked, which has sometimes meant I can be a bit of a chameleon in my efforts to try and fit in; I become different things to different people, trying to fit the mould of what I think they want. I can understand why people have called me an 'actress' in some situations, but this isn't a conscious decision.

The reality is, I can be a people-pleaser. So many of us are like this to some extent. We adapt and change depending on who we're speaking to. On a show like *Celebrity Big Brother*, though, this kind of behaviour is placed under a microscope. All your flaws become obvious for everyone to see. My tendency to people-please isn't necessarily a quality I like about myself, and it's one that I've tried to distance myself from by portraying myself as the strong, independent woman who doesn't care what people think. In reality, I do care. I really do. Little Ekin-Su tried her best to stay true to her authentic self while she was being bullied, but she still cared – and she would spend the next two decades shape-shifting in order to be liked.

To be honest with you, the *Big Brother* house reminded me of the *Love Island* villa in a lot of ways. The way the beds were laid out, the way the Diary Room was so similar in function to the Beach Hut, having no contact with the outside world . . . it felt very much alike. Maybe this seems obvious to you, but I hadn't really anticipated that. I didn't think the whole experience, which I was doing to separate myself from my *Love Island* beginnings, would actually take me back there. This meant I became defensive whenever anyone mentioned *Love Island*. Of course, I knew that this was where my reality TV career had begun; it's why most people know who I am, and I'm extremely grateful for all the opportunities I've had because of it. But it also reminded me of my ex.

Every time I thought about *Love Island*, I pictured Davide, and the hope I had that I'd found 'the one'. It wasn't just a game to me – it was the start of a relationship that had left me deeply hurt. The problem was, I hadn't processed any of this, or even admitted it to myself. So it was difficult to explain that to my fellow housemates. I also didn't want to talk about my ex very much while I was in the house. I was trying to escape it, rather than confronting it head-on. And so, whenever anyone mentioned *Love Island*, I became snappy and frustrated, as I was trying to distance myself from those memories. I've reflected on it a lot since leaving the house, and I'm aware of how that came across. Sometimes, you don't know why you've reacted in a certain way until you look back on it.

The same goes for the comment I made about how I would never use OnlyFans. Coming out of the house, I could see how this came across as snobby or judgemental. The truth is, this platform was such a sore spot for me because these were the girls to whom I was constantly comparing myself when I was in my relationship. My comment was a defence mechanism. I believed that if I distanced myself from the women who use OnlyFans, then maybe it would make me feel less inadequate. That has nothing to do with people who make money from platforms like OnlyFans. Everyone should do whatever feels right for them. My comment wasn't about them, it was about me, and my own insecurities. That's so often the case, isn't it? We all have our own unique histories, perspectives and traumas. It means we interpret information differently, and we have knee-jerk reactions without thinking things through.

There were a few other instances that ultimately led to my early eviction, but I don't want to relive everything that happened, or place blame on anyone or anything. I didn't always behave in the right way, but I'm only human, and we all make mistakes. In fact, I will continue to make mistakes – but hopefully they won't be the same ones I've made before. I know that I wasn't my usual bubbly, friendly self in that house. I wasn't the confident, empowered Ekin-Su that people knew from *Love Island*. And how could I have been? So much had changed in the year and a half since then. I had done several reality shows, which were amazing, but had also led to burnout and difficult times. I had gained followers, but lost friends. I'd had a turbulent relationship with my boyfriend, and a break-up that had left me brokenhearted. I was not healed by any stretch of the imagination. If anything, I needed help more than ever. I was sensitive, defensive and downtrodden. I needed to be grounded in reality, rather than playing a game. *Celebrity Big Brother* is definitely not the place to process heartbreak, let me tell you!

As I sat on the sofa on eviction night, hearing boos from the crowd whenever my name was mentioned by the hosts Will and AJ, my heart sank. *What had happened? What had I done?* I felt so confused, and more lost than ever. When my name was finally called as the latest person to be evicted, I knew it was coming. But I dreaded facing the public. I just wanted to curl up into a ball, hide away in a dark room and be on my own. I didn't want to go out there and plaster on a smile when I was crying on the inside. I tried to act normal as I said goodbye to everyone, but I couldn't look anyone in the face. I felt like I couldn't trust anyone. I couldn't trust myself. My distracted bubble had burst, and I knew I would have to face the music.

Thankfully, when the doors opened and I stepped outside on to the runway, the boos were drowned out by cheers. I thought: *OK, maybe I'm not as alone as I thought.* It was so overwhelming leaving the house, and all I wanted was a hug from my mum. I felt like a little kid again, and as soon as I saw her, I melted into her arms. She told me she loved me and to hold my head up high, which was just what I needed.

I only had five minutes between my eviction and my interview with AJ and Will. In this time, my loved ones told me: 'They've edited you really badly.'

Those words were echoing in my ears when I took my seat on the *Late & Live* show, which made me become even more defensive than I had been already. Sitting down in that chair was terrifying. I looked around at the crowd, and it felt like they were all giving me dirty looks. I don't know if this was just what was happening in my head, or if they actually were, but I felt paranoid, like I was the odd one out and everyone hated me. I had never felt as small in my life as I did during that interview. It's safe to say it did not go well!

Arriving home, I felt absolutely awful. The trolling and stories that had been published about me made me feel embarrassed, ashamed and so sad. I had experienced this kind of thing before, but for the first time since I'd been in the public eye, the negative feedback was overwhelming. I knew that I didn't want to attend the *Celebrity Big Brother* final because of how I was feeling. Despite some people telling me I should go, I decided to listen to myself in that moment. For the first time in my career, I told people, 'No.' At first, I worried what people would think of me. I imagined people saying: 'She's so pathetic, she can't even come back to the final.' But I knew I had to block out those voices with the sound of my own voice. It was a wake-up call that I needed to treat myself with more love, and to commit to my own needs and wants. I knew I had to start taking my own advice and really prioritise my healing journey. That was the day I learned what boundaries were, and what was right for me. I chose myself for the first time in my life, and I am incredibly proud of myself for standing by that decision. I was clear on what I needed to do, and it's one of my biggest accomplishments to date: being able, in that moment, to say, 'No.'

Reconnecting with Reality

A few days after leaving the *Big Brother* house, I knew I needed to take some time away to reflect. So I booked myself on to a wellness retreat abroad for a week. It involved yoga, eating healthily, workouts and beautiful hikes along the shoreline. I can't tell you how much I needed that experience. Stepping away for a few days helped me to rediscover who I was, beyond the TV persona and the social media posts. I was just Ekin-Su – for the first time in a really long time.

I barely went on my phone while I was there, and I found myself appreciating the beauty of nature. I noticed the sounds of the trees rustling in the wind, and the vibrant colours of all the flowers. It felt like I was tuning in to the world again, after such a long time of having everything on mute. During free time, I'd go and walk the streets of the nearby town, saying 'hello' to the locals, and buying fresh bread and tomatoes. It sounds so ordinary, but that's exactly what I needed – and what I loved. I wasn't worrying about posting anything on social media, or what people thought of me. Nobody recognised me there; I was just another visitor. I'd wander around with my headphones in my ears, listening to classical music. I love how classical music makes me feel – the way it washes over you and helps you drift away. I had been judged for liking classical music in my past relationships. Boyfriends had said it was weird. It felt good to just say: 'Who cares? I like it, so I'm going to listen to it.'

While I was there, I made time to write in a journal, and really reflect on what had happened over the past few weeks on *Celebrity Big Brother*. I knew I needed to take accountability for my actions. I know that I have a good heart and I didn't mean to hurt anyone, but I could understand why the viewers didn't agree with some of the things I did and said. I knew that I had been defensive. I knew that I could be cold. I knew that I hadn't been in the right state of mind to be there in the first place.

Part of growing up means reflecting on your actions. It's about thinking, *Maybe there are things I could've done differently*. We all make mistakes, but we can use every mistake as an opportunity to learn and grow. I'd thought I had it all figured out, but that wasn't true. In many ways, I was back at square one. Life is an ongoing journey, and I'm a work in progress – just like everyone else. I used to think being 'mature' meant you were a perfect person, but now I understand that it's about taking ownership of your personality and your flaws. It's about recognising that there are parts of yourself that still need to be worked on. Admitting when you're wrong is not a sign of weakness. It's actually a sign of strength. I didn't realise that before – but I know it now. If you deny your problems exist, then how will you be able to solve them?

I thought about my break-up, and I realised how experiences from my youth had shaped who I became in that relationship. I had struggled with setting boundaries and knowing what I deserved, thanks to the bullying I'd experienced at school and the toxic relationships I'd been in throughout my twenties. All I wanted was love and validation, and it meant I was willing to accept the bare minimum. It took me such a long time to end the relationship because I didn't trust my instincts, and my imagination overpowered my reality. I wanted so badly to believe in the fairy tale – I thought that maybe, if I wished for it enough, it would come true. But life isn't like that. I couldn't expect a man to swoop in and carry me off into the sunset. I needed to stop being so reliant on other people's love to validate me, and start looking for that same love within myself.

Coming back from the trip, I felt like a different person. It didn't completely heal me, of course – one week won't magically solve all your problems. But it set me off on the right path. And although you can't always run away for a week when the going gets tough, there are always mini ways in which you can escape your circumstances and reconnect with who you really are. Maybe that's a long walk in the forest near where you live. Maybe that's a whole weekend with your phone switched off. Sometimes you need to step back and look at your life from a distance, almost like you're watching a movie. Then you can think: *What is happening to that main character? What are they doing wrong? And how can I rewrite their story to make it even better?*

Life goes on, and I knew I needed to get back to work. I'm still grateful to be working in this industry, even though it can be a real roller coaster dealing with public opinion. I love so much of the work that I do. I adore my

BPerfect make-up range, and it makes me so happy to go to Belfast (where the brand is based) and meet fans. The first trip there after I returned from my retreat was really special. It reminded me that there are people out there who love and support me. When *Celebrity Big Brother* finished, it felt like the end of the world. I thought I would be cast as the villain for ever. But I know that the world moves on, and there's always an opportunity to come back stronger. It did make me realise, though, that I need to hold my own in this world. I need to take control of my own destiny, rather than allowing the industry to eat me up and swallow me whole. I have the power to change my role in my own story.

I also knew that I needed to accept the past. I can't go back and undo my relationship with Davide – and nor would I want to. That relationship (and the TV show it started on) changed my life, and brought me so many blessings. It also taught me a lot about myself, and the lines I need to draw in the sand in future relationships. I wish nothing but the best for Davide, and I'll always be grateful for the journey we went on together. In the same way, I knew I needed to accept the career path I had taken. I know now that I shouldn't have said 'yes' to *Celebrity Big Brother*, but the past is the past, and all I can do is look towards the future, and feel thankful for the lessons I've learned.

We will all go through times in life where we mess up, make bad decisions or feel like the world is against us. We can take accountability, while also acknowledging why we are the way we are, and knowing we are still worth something. We are still enough. You don't deserve to be defined by your mistakes, your flaws or your failures. You should be defined by how you move forward – how you pick yourself up, dust yourself off and say: 'It isn't over yet.'

Chapter 9

BE YOUR OWN BEST FRIEND

Recently, I have become best friends with a very special girl. She has actually been my friend since the day I was born, but we've had a love-hate relationship over the years. She hasn't always treated me very well. Sometimes, she'd tell me I looked ugly, or that no one would ever love me because I'm not blonde with fair skin. Or she'd say that there's a reason I haven't always had a lot of other friends, and it's because I'm a bad person. Recently, she has been a lot better. She keeps me company on long walks listening to classical music. She comes with me to the gym and reminds me to keep pushing – not because I need to lose weight, but because she knows it'll make me feel happier afterwards. She encourages me to get a good night's sleep, and warns me to stop reading the comments sections on articles with my name in the headline. She's honest with me and tells me the truth, but always in a kind and loving way. I know I can rely on her when I need her in tough times. I also know that, if everyone else tells me I'm amazing, she will keep me grounded and remind me that I'm still just an ordinary girl. Most of all, she loves me and I love her.

That friend is called Ekin-Su. That friend is me.

It's strange that we find it so much easier to be good friends to other people than we do to ourselves. We see all their best qualities, and we forgive them for their flaws. It's harder to do that for yourself, but it's something you have to keep on striving for every single day. You have to speak to yourself in the mirror (even though it might make you feel a bit silly in the process). Every time you have negative thoughts about yourself, you have to think: *What would I say, if my friend said this to me?* It takes a lot of practice, and it won't happen overnight. My best friend (aka me) can still occasionally be rude, or make me feel bad, but we're working on it.

If you want to become a better friend to yourself, here's a good exercise you can try: write yourself a letter. A psychologist recommended this to me, because it's a good way of pretending you're speaking to someone else. And then, when you read it back, it's like receiving a pep talk from someone who loves you. Knowing that you have this person within yourself can be extremely healing and inspiring.

I decided to write a letter to my younger self as a way of healing my inner child. We all have an inner child who we carry around with us throughout our lives. Even when we think we are all grown up, independent and empowered, we still have that child within us who is scared or vulnerable, or who is desperate for love or attention. Instead of ignoring the little Ekin-Su and pushing her away, I thought that speaking directly to her could help to heal me in some way. Maybe reading my letter will inspire you to write your own letter to your younger self. What would you say?

Dear ten-year-old Ekin-Su,

First of all, I want you to know that I see you. I understand how much you have struggled with moving to Essex, giving up dancing, the bullying at school, and being on your own at home. It's a lot for a child to deal with, and you're so brave and strong. I am really proud of you for holding your head up high and finding ways to comfort yourself and be happy in your own company. You won't always find this so easy as you get older – you'll look to others for comfort and happiness. But that's OK – it's only natural to seek love and affection. You won't always receive it in the way that you deserve, and sometimes you'll feel lonely, but you are resilient enough to get through those moments.

One thing I love about you is that you're wide-eyed and hopeful. You love fairy tales and romcoms, and you have faith that your life will turn out to be amazing, despite all the difficult things you're experiencing right now. In some ways, your life will become even more incredible than you ever imagined. You may not be liked by people at school, but soon you'll be liked by millions of people around the world! Just like Jenna Rink in your favourite movie, 13 Going on 30, you'll grow up to have some amazing and glamorous opportunities. You'll be on people's TV screens, you'll walk on red carpets, you'll have your picture taken at photoshoots, and you'll meet celebrities who know your name. There are so many exciting things to look forward to!

But also, like Jenna, you'll discover that life isn't perfect all the time. Sadly, there will be bad characters who come into your life disguised as good characters, and they'll take advantage of how trusting you are. People who are supposed to love you will hurt you. I know that sometimes, you'll find it hard to spot these bad actors. They'll criticise you or try to control you, but then they'll cover it up by saying they love you and they're only looking out for you. Please know that if someone loved you, they wouldn't make you continually prove your worth. They wouldn't make you shrink yourself – they would want you to grow and bloom like a flower. Please know that happiness doesn't come from fame, money, or the seemingly 'perfect' boyfriend. Happiness comes from the inside, and you should always stay committed to finding your own happiness.

Unfortunately, your idea of love will become intertwined with anxiety, but I want you to know that you deserve more love than you'll be given. The other person's behaviour has nothing to do with you and whether you are enough. However, every person who comes into your life is there for a reason – to teach you something. You'll learn new things every step of the way. The bad relationships will be hard, but they're just stepping stones until you get to where you're meant to be.

I know you feel insecure about how you look, especially when you look around and see 'beautiful' girls who look nothing like you. Over the years, you will try and change how you look with dieting, make-up, fillers and surgery that will leave physical scars. I understand why you want that, because it's so hard feeling 'ugly' and different to everyone else. But I want you to know that you are enough, and you are beautiful, exactly as you are.

'Beauty' isn't what you think it is. It's not all about visuals, like what you see when you look in the mirror, or the image of a handsome husband, or the way your life looks from the outside. Beauty has a much wider definition, and over the years, you'll come to appreciate all of it. When you're lying on the beach and looking out at the vast ocean – that's beauty. When the waiter brings your favourite dessert over to the table – that's beauty. When someone makes you laugh – that's beauty. It comes from your soul and the way you look at life. Your emotions are beautiful, too – even the negative ones. It's OK to let yourself feel everything, because it's part of being human.

You should also know that fashions will change constantly. I know it feels like you'd be the coolest person ever if you had a velour tracksuit and a designer bag right now, but styles come and go. You might think having a big bum is 'bad', but in a few years, people will celebrate big bums. You might think that there's something wrong with being hairy, but in a few years, lots of people will let their body hair grow out on purpose! Being 'different' might feel like a problem to you, but when you're older, being unique will be much more celebrated. Diversity is more interesting than everyone looking the same. Ideas of what is cool, beautiful and fashionable change all the time. What matters is the person you are inside. Your personality, your values, your morals... that stuff never goes out of season.

Of course, you'll change and grow as you get older – but always hold on to what makes you who you are. Never stop belting out eighties pop songs in the bathroom. Never stop dancing around the kitchen listening to classical music. Never stop being fun, playful and giddy – and try to surround yourself with people who bring out that side of you. Being an adult might become more stressful, with all the responsibilities and big changes, but you'll still be a little kid deep down – and there's nothing wrong with that.

I hate to say that you will go through some things in your life that are too difficult and traumatic to even talk about in this book. You will make mistakes and bad decisions, and fail a lot along the way. But every low moment will teach you something, and you'll come back even braver and stronger.

I'm sorry that I haven't always been the best friend to you. I have reaffirmed other people who have told you that you're not good enough, not pretty enough and not cool enough. I have said those words to you as well, and I apologise for being so mean. I will spend the rest of my life trying to make it up to you. You don't have to be perfect in order to be loved.

I love you,
Ekin-Su xxx

Looking to the Future

Sometimes you need to look backwards in order to move forwards. Now that I've acknowledged the little girl inside me, I can start thinking about my future. I can think about all the ways in which I hope I'll grow and become an even better friend to myself.

One of my biggest goals is to be a role model to young people. I love meeting fans at meet-and-greets, and I have been into schools to do talks. I'd love to do more of that, because I know how it feels to be young, lost and insecure, and I wish I could've had someone give me advice like a big sister. I want young people to know all the things I told my younger self in my letter. I want to tell them that they should always hold tight to their dreams, but that it's OK to be imperfect and make poor decisions along the way. I would love to write books for kids, and work with more charities and organisations that protect children from bullying. I want to use my experiences to help others. I think that would be so rewarding.

I know that part of being a good role model means practising what I preach. I hope that the future-me will learn to make peace with her appearance. Over the years, I have tried bending and shaping myself into the most beautiful woman possible, but I hope my future-self feels a lot more comfortable in her own skin, and knows that she doesn't *need* to change anything. It can take a lot of inner work to undo all the negative feelings you have about yourself. I'm nowhere near there yet, but I hope I will embrace myself more and more as I get older.

I'm not exactly where I want to be in my life right now, but I hope that my future-self is still following her dreams of acting and presenting. I would love to be in a series on Netflix, or to present a documentary about something that is important to me. I'm so grateful for all the things reality TV has given me, but it has never been my end goal to be a reality TV person. I'm still that ambitious, big dreamer I was when I was a little kid. I want to keep challenging myself and looking for new dreams. I hope I never lose that.

In the same way, I hope I will prioritise the jobs and opportunities that mean something to me. I want to do more of what I love, without a fear of being judged. I don't want to do things just because people around me tell me that they're a good idea. I hope I get better at setting clear boundaries, telling people 'no' and trusting my gut instinct. I hope I can listen to the little voice in my head – my own best friend – rather than letting it get drowned out by all the outside chatter. I hope I can learn to trust myself, rather than always seeking advice from others. Of course, we all need second opinions every once in a while, but I want to get better at tuning in to my own thoughts and opinions. I hope future-me becomes more comfortable showing my truest, most vulnerable self to the world. I don't always have to act like I'm independent and nothing phases me. I can show sides of myself that I might have thought were shameful before. I hope I will find a way to let go of some of that shame.

In an ideal world, I would love future-me to be surrounded by people who love and respect her. I'd love her to have a kind and caring husband. But I also have to focus on the relationship I have with myself. I need to fill up my own love cup before I can expect anyone else to fill it. Whether my future-self is in a relationship or not, I hope she'll be happy most of the time. I hope she's constantly learning new things about herself, improving on past flaws and learning from mistakes. I want the absolute best for the Ekin-Su of the future – and I feel the same about you.

The Most Important Relationship You'll Ever Have

When this book comes out, I will have just turned thirty years old. When I watched my favourite movie, *13 Going on 30*, and imagined myself at this age, I always thought I would feel so grown up, and that my life would have clicked into place. But the reality is, that never actually happens. I thought I had achieved everything when I won *Love Island*, but I didn't know that the journey was just beginning. Going into my thirties, I know that it's just another chapter of my story. I don't know what the future holds, but I feel excited and hopeful about the journey.

I hope you have gained something from reading this book. I have tried my best to share my advice and lessons along the way – from my school years, right up to my time on reality TV – all geared towards helping you improve your relationship with yourself (while I also try to take my own advice!). But if you take away just one thing from this book, I want it to be this: you have everything you need within yourself. You are enough, and you're worthy, just as you are. You don't need to change everything about yourself. You don't need to squeeze yourself into boxes just to make other people approve of you. You don't need to be anything other than yourself.

This doesn't mean you shouldn't take accountability for your mistakes and work on improving your flaws. It's just that self-improvement should always come from *you*, and what you know deep down is best for you. It's all about building a better life for yourself rather than waiting for other people to do it for you, or wanting someone else to validate you and tell you that you're doing a good job. Everything in the world moves and changes, comes and goes. But you always have YOU. Yes, you will go through hard times, but you will have magical times too. Even when everything feels awful, never give up hope that magic times are ahead. Even when you feel lonely, never forget that YOU are the best company.

A best friend is someone who makes you feel like you're not alone. Someone who supports you, has your back and brings out the best in you. They're someone you can lean on, someone who will be honest with you and tell you the truth, even if it's something you don't want to hear. You can have all these qualities – and more. You just have to look within yourself, and there they are!

I'm still on this crazy roller coaster that is life, and I know there will be many highs, lows and topsy-turvy moments coming further down the tracks. But now I know that, throughout all of that, I will always have myself to lean on. I can squeeze my own hand and say, 'It's going to be all right.'

Because it is. It really is.

RESOURCES

Here are the contact details of organisations that offer useful information and help on some of the topics discussed in this book.

Mind: a leading mental health charity which provides mental health information, support and online communities
www.mind.org.uk

British Association for Counselling and Psychotherapy (BACP): provides information and details on how to find a therapist
www.bacp.co.uk

Relate: organisation offering information and support on relationships and sex
www.relate.org.uk

National Bullying Helpline: a charity that offers advice and support to adults as well as children
www.nationalbullyinghelpline.co.uk
Helpline: 0300 323 0619

Beat Eating Disorders: Beat provides information and support to those affected by eating disorders
www.beateatingdisorders.org.uk

Samaritans: provides emotional support to anyone in the UK suffering emotional distress, struggling to cope or at risk of suicide
www.samaritans.org
Helpline: 116 123

ACKNOWLEDGEMENTS

Thank you to all the team who have helped me to tell my story in a safe space. Thank you to my wonderful publishers for your patience, understanding and for allowing me to take ownership of my book. Coming into this project I never imagined how life changing opening up could be – it's made me realise how strong I am, and how much learning and reflecting I still must do. Thank you to Zoe, Oscar, Arielle, Jillian, Narjas and Brionee, who have shown me consideration and kindness throughout this process, particularly during times of struggle and sadness, which I have been able to talk about in the book. I have worked with the team on the book throughout my most vulnerable moments, and, in my darkest days, I have felt so grateful to my team for standing by me, and for believing in me when I haven't believed in myself. Writing this book has taken me to places I haven't wanted to revisit in a long time, but it has been necessary as part of my healing.

Thank you to anybody who continues to show support and love to me, you are always seen, and you will always have an important place in my heart. I feel so blessed to have the most loyal followers, who love me for being me. To my family, who continue to love and protect me always, thank you. I hope I continue to make you proud. I wouldn't be here without you.

To the TV shows, production companies and channels who have taken me under their wing, thank you for giving me the opportunities that have enabled me to pursue my dreams.

To the bullies and to those who caused me sadness and pain, I hope you have found happiness. I wish you peace and love, and I forgive you.

To the volunteers and charities who continue to support people who are struggling, I am in awe of the work that you do. Thank you for your continued work and care for those who are feeling lost and broken. In our darkest days, it's your teams that become the lights at the end of a dark tunnel.

To Little Ekin-Su, this book wouldn't have been possible without you. I am proud of us for telling our story and for taking back control of our story. I am the woman I am today because of you, and I love you.